MW01236043

The Shaping of a Vital Black Man Child:

A Rite of Passage Project

By
Rogers W. Jackson

Airleaf Publishing

airleaf.com

ISBN: 1-60002-054-2

Acknowledgements

I want to thank the Chief Men
who made this project possible.

The Men of First Baptist
University Park, Illinois

Rudolph Hudnell
Michael Williams
Lester Scarborough III
Carl West, Johnny Polk
John Rodgers, Terrance Threatt
Roosevelt Collins, Gregory Sutton
Svend Tranberg, Jimmie Young
Larry Whitehead, Michael Whitted
Jimmie Weatherspoon, Michael Spight

Men who have Mentored Me

McKinley Brister
Len Fuller, Jr.
Lester Beene
Dr. P.W. Thompson
Dr. John Mangram
Dr. Kenneth Smith
Dr. Lee Butler, Jr.
Dr. Robert Moore

Special Assistant
William B. Wyatt

"It isn't [***so terrible being a timid man***]
if you are going to be immortal, but if
you are going to die there is no time for timidity."
(Moore & Gillette, 1993, p. 116)

Special Thanks
Rev. Donald Williams
Rev. Stanley Williams
Rev. E. Ray Bynam
Rev. George Cook, Jr.
Rev. L. K. Curry
Dr. Michael A. Bell

"I searched for a man
among them who would
repair the wall and
stand in the gap."
(Ezekiel 22:30)

My Mission

Develop a few men who will make a difference in the life of Black Male Children.

Man Child Objectives

1. Give boys a sense of ***"Mission and Calling"*** that focuses on a central task.

2. Develop ***self-discipline*** in boys to achieve skills in both body, mind, and emotions.

3. Become ***faithful*** and loyal to the church, work, home, and family.

4. Recognize the ***urgency*** of the moment and do not waste time nor talent.

5. ***Defend what is just and true*** and stand against what wounds, damages, causes despair, depression, injustice, and oppression.

(See Moore & Gillette, 1993, pp. 110-116)

"Effective leadership requires [the] strength of [a] few men [who] are able to access or steward responsibility"
(Moore & Gillette, 1993, p. 109)

Contents

Introduction

The Criminalization or the Christianization of the Black Man Child

In a Thursday, August 25, 2005 news article titled, "Black Murder Stat Doubtful, but Cause for Alarm Anyway," Mary Mitchell (2005), a Chicago Sun Times staff writer observed a serious concern about the number of "Black on Black" murders that are taking place. It was suggested by one statistician that Blacks are "seven times more likely to commit murder than whites" (p. 10). In an article titled, "Too Many Rappers Dying for a Shot at Fame," Richard Roeper (2005, p. 11), lists in the August 30, 2005 issue of the Chicago Sun Times young Black "hip hop" rappers whose bullet wounds were "badges of credibility" and death.

Look at the following list of the "Black Man Child"(dren) who are gone because of violent crimes: ***50 Cents*** was shot nine times and lived to tell the tale, but others did not make it – In 1999, ***Lamont Coleman*** (Big L, 24) killed in a drive-by, in 2000, Rap Producer ***Ronald Blackburn*** shot and killed, in 2001, ***McKinley "Mac Da Assassin" Phipps*** convicted of manslaughter, in 2002, in 2003, ***Corey "C-Murder" Miller*** kills a 16 year old, in 2003, Hip-hop executive ***Bernard Harris*** is shot and killed, in 2003, ***Freaky Zeeky*** is wounded and a friend is killed in a drive-by, in 2004 Robert Montanez is shot to death, in 2005 ***Rapper Beelow*** is hospitalized after being shot in the head (Roeper, 2005, p. 11). Roeper (2005) concludes his article with the words,

> So it goes. Young, black men make the music, live the life and kill each other. Young blacks – and many more young whites – buy the music and blast it from their car stereos, nodding their heads and singing along to the tough guy lyrics. Older blacks – and many more older whites – own the labels and get rich from the music. And the hits, musical and other wise, just keep on coming" (p. 11).

The question of whether "Black on Black" murders are higher than "white on white murders" can be seen when "another Black man is gone" and we keep on going as though nothing happened. If Black men are killing each other at a higher rate than other ethnic groups, it only points us to a serious realization. The realization is that "Black men" and boys are in a crisis situation. Each day the Black man and the Black man child are being placed into the criminal justice system and prison industrial complexes at a higher rate than other ethnic groups. The question before us is whether we will be Christians or criminals?

Black men and boys have been labeled as "predators," "victimizers," and now we are the "criminalized." The stigma of being seen as criminals is horrendous. Yet, in the media, videos, music, and the movies, we are the "gangsters," "the Boyz in the Hood," and the "Menaces to Society." The ***"criminalization" of the Black man*** in the media is a real problem that is not being addressed (Mitchell, 2005, p. 10).

The challenge before us in this study is to begin the process of the ***"Christianization" of Black men*** and boys. Throughout the Bible, there is a call from being a "sinner" (criminal) to becoming a "saint." Black men first begin as Black boys. To drastically reduce the "criminalization" of the Black man, we must increase the "Christianization" of Black boys.

To "Christianize" Black boys, we must engage in the methodology of our Lord Jesus Christ who gave us the ***"Rite of Passage Paradigm"*** in the "Follow Me" passages.

Into Life: Read and discuss what it means to follow Jesus versus following the crowd.

Read **Matthew 4:19-20**. What does the Lord want us to become?

____

Read **Matthew 16:24-25**. What does it mean to deny yourself and follow Jesus?

____

Read **Mark 8:34**. To follow Christ means to take up a cross daily. What is the cross we must take up?

____

Read **Luke 9:59ff**. To follow Jesus means to take hold of a plow and not look back. What is the Lord calling us to do in this level of followship? ________________

____

Part 1: Leave No Black Boy Behind

The question of this study has to do with the "social location" of black boys in American society. In the socio-cultural, socio-economic, socio-political, and socio-religious context, where do black boys stand? How are black boys identified and defined in each of the above contexts?

The major concern of Black men is to engage in critical dialogue to denounce the alienation black boys experience and promote interdependent and interactive relationships among men and boys that strive to constructively challenge, meet the needs, concerns, and interests of black boys. How can this interaction transform and liberate black boys to a viable Black manhood?

Some of the ***key concerns of leaving no black boy behind*** is 1) developing a system of accountability, 2) dialoguing with and listening to boys who have been excluded and left behind, and 3) affirming their "otherness," their interests and concerns (see Segovia & Tolbert, 1995, p. 39-40).

The problems black boys face are multidimensional. They are black males in a white male dominated world; they are adolescent, between childhood and adulthood; they are in identity confusion, not knowing who they are nor where they stand in the world; they are given a "script" of behavior and a role to play and follow as black boys. For them to go outside the social scripting is to face opposition and judgment (see Segovia & Talbert, 1995, p. 62).

Because black boys will not follow the "script" given to them by society, they have been defined and labeled as lazy, destructive, (un)enterprising, carefree, undisciplined, violent, vulgar, and unintelligent. Black boys are "strangers" and undesirables that are to be kept outside the social arena (see Segovia & Tolbert, 1995, p. 63). To illustrate the above considerations, a Wednesday, January 14, 2004 issue of the Chicago Sun Times article was titled – "1 in 4 Boys in foster Care Get Charged with Crimes." Fusco (2004) noted,

> One in four Cook County boys who enter the state's foster-care system end up accused of crimes in juvenile court./ Also, the more often boys move between homes within foster care, the more likely they are to have run-ins with police.
>
> The more boys moved within foster care, the more likely they were to end up being involved in criminal activity (p. 31).

In his visionary novella, Rite of Passage, Richard Wright (1994) predicted about fifty years ago the plight of Black foster boys who fell into juvenile delinquency, and violent crime in the urban ghettos of America (Rampersad, 1994, p. 118). The tragedy that Black boys face in the foster care system stemmed partly from social conditions and social systems that produce alienation and rage in young Black males (Rampersad, 1994, p. 119).

In a Chicago Sun Times article titled, "Schools Pressured to Dump Bad Students," the story reported that Black male Chicago High School students are being dropped from school for skipping classes and getting into trouble. One student that was dropped stated,

> "I'm not one to blame others for what I did, but if the school had steered me the right way, it could have helped."/ "A lot of students just give up. It's almost like their life has no direction, they ain't got nothing going" (Grossman, 2004, p. 8).

In the 2001 through 2002 school year, 17,400 students dropped out of the Chicago School System, even with the 27 alternative school set up in the city to assist them. Schools are pressured to push out truant, low-performing students because they are not meeting the testing requirements and the attendance benchmarks set by the State Education Committee (Grossman, 2004, p. 8).

One of the basic challenges we face is to "Leave No Black Boy Behind." Our challenge is to slow down the "push out program" and help them go the "extra mile" and stay in school, the family, and the church. The process must begin through public, private, and parochial preschools and through academic support for middle school and high school freshmen who have the greatest difficulty. We must give our boys another opportunity.

In addressing the plight of black males today, Richard Wright (1994), in 1945 began to address psychological, economic, racial, and political stresses that affect the black family and black boys. In Rite of Passage, he writes of Johnny, a foster child, who runs away from home because "the city" (the system) moved him from his foster family of fifteen years for no reason. The authorities insisted that Johnny, a fifteen years old, had to be sent to a new home.

According to Wright (1994), the uncaring, nameless, and faceless system drove him to join and become the leader of a gang. He was tested in a fight. He lost his innocence. He transitioned from a child to a man. He became known as "the Jackal" and the leader of the gang. Subconsciously, he wanted someone to call him home, to stop him, but there was no man to help him.

The problem the novella explores is the ***psychology of alienation and loneliness*** faced by Black males that leads to the high drop out rates and violence. In the story, Johnny is dominated by love from his stepmother and stepsister, but little love and attention from adult Black males. His stepfather is absent during his break with the family. The stepfather is a shadowy figure who does not have the influence to stop Johnny from running away (Rampersad, 1994, p. 125).

The message of Wright's (1994) Rite of Passage centers on the plight of Black manhood as represented in the four boys in the story "Baldy, Skinkie, Treetop, and Johnny." There is a waste of human energy in idleness. These boys represents Black boys and men who are seen in society as "mutants" (Rampersad, 1994, pp. 129-130). The challenge of Rite of Passage is a call to Black men, the church, schools, courts, and other institutions to respond to the crisis of Black juvenile delinquency, push out and drop out rates in schools that lead to delinquency. How can broken boys be rehabilitated and given a chance?

In the close of the story, Johnny and the gang rob a white man. Johnny believes he sees a Black woman observing them and she calls out, "YOU BOYS! YOU BOYS!" The answer to the plight of Black boys is in those of us who have eyes to see and observe. We must see what is happening and call out to our sons, "YOU BOYS! YOU BOYS!" We must capture their attention, their time, and their energy for the benefit of the culture. You and I must demand a solution and become the solution by being the Elder Mentors.

A. The Challenge of Black Men: Build Relationships with Black Boys

Black boys are left behind because Black men will not surround them. Black boys need to be protected and surrounded by Black men so that they can grow to become mature men. One of the problems in Black male development is the loss of the experience of relationships. Women in our society are largely responsible for early child care (Gilligan, 1993, p. 7). One of the challenges of today is to develop early childhood "man care" centers.

1. The Heroic Stage of Boyhood

In the early days of a black boy's development, he gains his identity from his mother or the female to whom he is associated and attached. In the beginning, he defines himself in relation and connection to the feminine personality rather than the male personality (see Gilligan, 1993, p. 7).

After the boy moves from childhood into adolescence, he notes a varied difference between him and his mother or female care giver. The boy recognizes that he cannot fuse with the female; he realizes that he is the opposite of the female and begins the process of separation from the mother, thus curtailing his "primary love and empathic tie" (Gilligan, 1993, p. 8) to find one "like him," to whom he can identify and gain definition for his being.

Moore & Gillette (1992), in <u>The Warrior Within</u>, observe that "masculine identity" and "self-definition" takes a lot of work. To discover his self-identity, a boy must "break with an overly empathetic tie to [the] mother and her ways of being and doing" (p. 103). In phases, the boy must reject the "feminine qualities" of "the power of the mother" (Moore & Gillette, 1992, p. 103). The power and fear of his mother that he must overcome is the "fear of sarcasm, ridicule, criticism, and depreciating remarks. Underlying these fears is the fear of being drawn back into a symbiotic merger with the all-powerful mother" (Moore & Gillette, 1992, p. 102). The boy becomes a hero when he makes the break with the identity with his mother and discovers himself and his masculine power and its limits (Moore & Gillette, 1992, p. 104).

2. *Gaining Black Male Identity*

Black men must surround black boys to help them experience their difference from the female and gain their masculine individuality and identity. What must Black men do so that no Black boy will be left behind? Black men must engage boys through education, projects, recreation, and play to teach basic skills of independence, cooperation, and caring. Develop educational programs and projects to teach the following—

1. Educationally, develop a "man care" curriculum that discusses—

    a. How to get ahead economically?
    b. How to obtain a "voice" in a culture that desires your silence?
    c. How to gain self-definition versus being defined by someone else?
    d. How to manifest a destiny of self-confidence, self-expression, and self-determination?
    e. How to revision and reclaim the future? (see Segovia & Tolbert, 1995, pp. 64-66).

2. Develop programs and processes that take black boys into social and personal relationships to mentor, teach, and to instruct them in family and community building activity.

3. Create recreational opportunities to:

    a. Teach boys to learn and respect rules.
    b. Explain competition and cooperation.
    c. Enhance skill development and productivity.
    d. Engage boys in how to debate, dispute, resolve quarrels, and resume play.
    e. Guide boys in being sensitive and caring.
    f. Develop organizational skills and coordination of activities.
    g. Explore independence, interdependence, and social control.
    h. Instruct boys how to love work, how to be industrious, how to be initiating, and how to be autonomous (see Gilligan, 1993, pp. 9-12).

B. Will Black Boys Have Faith?

What is faith? Faith has been defined as a "leap into the arms of Jesus." Faith is more than knowing about Jesus externally; it is ***knowing Jesus internally*** by being in relationship with Him (Dean, 2004, p. 150). Faith is turning to God completely in trust and faithfulness (Bromiley, 1985, p. 849. Faith comes by "hearing…the word of God" (Romans 10:17).

Faith when it is received through the word of God calls us to a response. Faith, according to John Goldingay (1995, pp. 7-8), calls us to an "implicit invitation" to love, to hope, to repent, to obey, and to worship. Faith is more than the dispensing of information; it is a call to "effect something" (Goldingay, 1995, p. 8) and do something in us. As a result of faith, we begin to "do something" in our world.

Will the Black male child have a faith that will do something in him and move him to do something in the world?

1. Faith Development through Preaching and Teaching

Transformative faith is a faith that calls us to "do and be something" different than what we are. The ***church pastor*** must play a ***role in the faith development*** of the Black male child through intentional and invitational preaching and teaching that moves the Black male child to "do something."

The transformative power of the faith is continued in the doctrines we teach and through the ***retelling of the story*** in the new situations. The shape, form, and our identity in the Christian faith is continued through our teaching and preaching the rituals, traditions, symbols, and customs, in our play, our words, our actions, and our relationships to others (Seymour & Miller, 1982, pp. 55, 56).

Romans 10:11 affirms that "faith" is cultivated through preaching. Preaching helps to ignite faith. John Goldingay (1995) states that the goal of preaching is "to do something to people: to engender or to deepen the response of faith" (p. 7).

According to Goldingay (1995), preaching calls us to respond to God. The faithful preacher must call young Black men to a faith that "responds to God," thus ***affecting something*** in their lives (Goldingay, 1995, p. 8). Transformative faith moves us to ***do something*** for God, and others. Faithful preaching calls young men on a journey that leads to growth, change, development, and a responsibility to assist others, who are on their journey to wholeness.

The ***curriculum of preaching and teaching*** should include 1) God's word that ***speaking to the darkness***, fear, uncertainty, and identity of young Black males (Genesis 1:3). Preaching and teaching should 2) bring ***freedom and liberation*** to the Black male child to grow and develop in a hostile world that is bent on their limitation, captivity, imprisonment, and destruction. Both should 3) ***offer an identity*** of newness and possibility (Jeremiah 1:4-5). This new "being" and identity (2 Corinthians 5:17) gives opportunity for esteem, place, and productivity in the church, home, school, and workplace. The preaching and teaching ministry of the pastor should 4) ***give direction*** to young Black males as to the contributions, creativity, business, and ministry that they are capable of developing and achieving (Smith, 2004, pp. 28-29).

2. *Faith Development through Vision Casting*

If our male children are to have faith, someone must give them a ***vision of their possibility***. Where there is no vision, young Black males perish (Proverbs 29:18). If our Black males are to have faith, it must be a faith that has as its foundation a vision of possibility to young men. Vision leads enables young Black boys to see what they cannot see (Read Deut. 31:7-8). We must help the young see that God can use the ordinary individual to do extraordinary things (Read 2 Kings 22). Faith enables us to encourage "kids who are scared, shy and intimidated…to go public with their gifts and speak boldly" (Smith, 2004, p. 15).

Efrem Smith (1994), in his book Raising Up Young Heroes observes that we must make strategic plans to help young people see that they can deal with the issues of their lives. They have the power to "bring love, justice, peace and transformation to the world" (Smith, 2004, p. 17).

The young Black male child can bring a positive change, and a "down-the-road impact" on what is affecting the community when they are given a vision.

One reason for our lack of activity and revolution is ***no articulated vision*** of how to get the job done. It is imperative that older adults become vision casters. We must articulate to them that God wants to use them in a great venture. Vision casting can establish a fire in young black males to motivate them to build the kingdom of Christ through love, purpose, and Spirit filled empowerment (Smith, 2004, pp. 19-20).

3. Faith Development through a Holistic Approach

Faith development is measured through "measurable outcomes." A retired Christian educator and principal, Mr. McKinnley Brister, of the Emmanuel Christian School, Chicago Illinois, told me in 2001 that children are best developed through the "Holistic Approach" of learning. If young Black males are to be developed, we must develop a ***holistic approach*** versus a ***program approach*** to their growth.

Our challenge as Christian educators and mentors of young Black men is to determine our strategic plans and our means of implementing them in the lives of young men. A holistic curriculum to help young men must include how we will affect their 1) ***praise and worship*** of the Lord. 2) In what ways will their ***emotions*** be involved, changed, and challenged in the process? 3) How will their ***bodies*** be brought under the control of Christ? 4) In what way will their ***mind and thoughts*** be enlightened toward positive outcomes? (Smith, 2004, pp. 36 - 37).

According to Efrem Smith (2004), the ***holistic approach*** is a lifelong journey of experiencing God's love, grace, and relationship. The holistic approach moves through event-orientations to proactive engagements in the work of the Lord (pp. 38-39). What must be the ***ongoing holistic biblical gospel curriculum*** to help Black male children become men? Smith (2004) affirms,

> Ultimately we are called to raise up disciples. Discipleship is about spiritual growth and maturity./ Jesus is about salvation, and we should not belittle this point in any way./ A holistic approach to [black male] ministry allows us a better opportunity to develop disciples and raise up young heroes for God" (p. 48).

Smith (2004, pp. 39-48) suggests the following as part of the holistic approach to ministry with the Black male child. The foregoing ideas must be long-term goals to reach the body, mind, and soul of the young man. To have an impact, the discussion must be centered on the biblical foundations of the word of God in the gospel.

1. Discuss ***personal issues*** young men are facing.

2. Encourage ***private retreats to be with God*** and reflect on the experience.

3. Develop ***academic centers*** to support/ enrich school work and homework.

4. Create ***sharing times*** where young men can "let off steam," be listened to without ridicule, and receive help in understanding their emotions.

5. Provide time for young men to ***share their stories***, pains, and frustrations.

6. Develop ***partnerships for counseling*** to help young men with serious issues.

7. Promote ***think tanks*** to help young men think through what they are going through at home and school.

8. Discuss ***health issues*** and health care for young men.

9. Address the ***issues of social life*** and how young men can glorify Christ.

10. Talk about the ***concerns of sexuality*** and body issues that boys have.

11. Need to be productive through work and vocation.

12. Discuss the need of salvation central to young men's spirituality.

13. Issues with "transcending" and ***dealing with racism*** (Winbush, 2001, p 43).

4. Faith Development through the Warrior Method

Raymond Winbush (2001), in his extraordinary work titled, The Warrior Method: A Parent's Guide to Rearing Healthy Black Boys offers a significant insight in how the Black male child's faith is developed. From observation, the Black male child's faith and understanding are ***negatively shaped*** by:

1. Role models shape Black male's self-image. Role models often serve as a means of fatherly acceptance and guidance.

2. The media affects Black boys through their imitation of negative and denigrative traits and vocabulary that is learned at an early age.

3. A system of racist thought that is not determined to educate Black children Winbush, 2001, pp. 51-52).

The ***positive shaping of the Black male child*** is witnessed in a curriculum that celebrates Black culture in "rite of passage" ceremonies, art, music, books, museums, Black churches, Black colleges, and values that reflect strength and courage of Black people (Winbush, 2001, pp. 52-53).

To positively shape the Black male child, the following can be done within the family and church structure:

A. Educate Black boys through workshops, service learning, reading, and play.

B. Emphasize Black history to help Black boys locate themselves psychologically in history.

C. Read thirty minutes a day on Black culture and life to understand the culture and history from which you emerge (Winbush, 2001, pp. 56-59).

D. Take Black boys to the Black church to help them grow spiritually in faith (Winbush, 2001, p. 59.

In her thought provoking book, Real Kids, Real Faith, Karen M. Yust (2004, pp. xxi - xxiii) further explains why going to church is necessary to cultivate faith. At church you—

1. Gain purpose and mission.
2. Explore a community of faithful people.
3. Obtain a spiritual formation and acquisition of language and ritual.
4. Encounter positive role models.
5. Experience leadership.
6. Encounter community and extended family.
7. Become socialized in the principles of love, acceptance, and compassion.
8. Participate in a community that promotes trusting relationships, building esteem, and

life-long opportunities to experience a life of faith.

Kendra Dean (2004), in her book, Practicing Passion asserts that best method to insure young men continue in the church after they are "big enough" to not be made to go, is by 1) ***cultivating their faith*** by training them in the home, 2) through devotional studies and Bible readings, and 3) allowing them to ***participate in the community of faith*** where they will be encouraged to internalize the beliefs and practices of the community (p. 146).

Raymond Winbush (2001) in The Warrior Method (2001) stipulates that "the healthy passage of black males from boyhood to manhood [is a] ***fight*** to accomplish" (p. 53). If our Black male children are to have faith, we cannot expect others to be their "saviors." We must ***fight and develop*** a curriculum of ***"advocacy"*** and ***"intercession"*** (Winbush, pp. 54-55). We cannot wait for "others" to teach our male children what it means to be a man in this culture that is bent on their destruction. For what must we ***fight to insure*** that our male children will have ***faith***?

1. Develop self-made and create curriculum that encourages individual expression and creativity.

2. Include in the curriculum positive adult roles of Black [s]heroes.

3. Present media materials and cultural events that enhance esteem.

4. Encourage schools, churches, and social agencies to assist Black males.

5. Work with Black lawyers who will argue and advocate justice (Winbush, 2001, pp. 54-55).

My faith, as an adult, moves me to "aid [young men] in the transition from despair to hope" (Pearson, 1989, pp. 33, 41). My faith enables me to get young Black males "unstuck" from themselves, their problems, their self-defeating behavior, and it frees them to move on a journey from self-involvement toward a responsibility of helping others (Pearson, 1989, pp. 44, 45).

How does the church nurture faith in Black males? The faith of young Black males is ***cultivated when they are welcomed*** into the faith life of the church. We can ***welcome the Black male child into faithfulness*** through the following suggestions:

1. Have intergenerational worship.
2. Include their experiences in sermons.
3. Include them in public prayers.
4. Sing intergenerational songs and music.
5. Have them among the church greeters and service.

6. Work in the community to improve their lives.
   a. Summer lunch programs
   b. Enrichment camps
   c. Programs to encourage esteem
   d. Tutoring programs
   e. Providing safe places after school (Yust, 2004, pp. 166, 168, 169, 170):

5. Faith Development through the Community of Faith

The challenge of the community of faith is to ***influence the content and character*** of the Black male child's faith commitment. The values and practices of the Christian ***faith are to be passed on through socializing events***—that seek to "build up" young Black males. The ***faith*** **must be** passed on through the ***"hidden curriculum"*** of the worship, the rituals, traditions, nurture, hymn-singing, and support. The community of faith must pass to the next generation of young men ***the faith*** that they might explore its implications and accept its meaning for use in their experience (Seymour & Miller, p. 59; Yust, p. 21).

A. ***The goal of the Christian Education for Black males:***
   1. Shaping attitudes and behaviors.
   2. Enable students to appropriate the faith into their contemporary situation (Seymour & Miller, p. 60).

B. ***How should we teach the faith?***
   1. Teach dialogically – teacher and student exchanging ideas, new visions, and new insights on biblical themes.
   2. Introduce biblical stories until they become a part of the thinking and acting of the learner.
   3. Link the stories to respond to the demands of contemporary events (Seymour & Miller, pp. 61, 62).
   4. Teach the faith as a ***multisensory experience***: physically through senses, emotionally, and socially (Yust, p. 8).
   5. Become familiar with the images and the characters of the faith.
      a. Know the name of the characters and personalities.
      b. Hear the stories of Jesus.
      c. Embrace the story through drama (Yust, pp. 24, 42).

C. ***What is the curriculum of the community of faith?*** The content of Christian education must include—
   1. The church's heritage, rituals, traditions, and lifestyles.
   2. The ancient faith and holidays.

3. The wisdom of the community of faith to live responsibly and creatively.
4. The stories, narratives, and songs found in the Bible in new ways.
5. Putting the stories of scripture in their own words and experience.
5. Teach formal prayers, oratories, artistic creations (Seymour & Miller, pp. 64-67; Yust, pp. 12, 29, 31, 49, 64, 66).

D. Teach ***faith as transformative***. When we come into the fellowship of the community of faith, we are called to be faithful. Faith not only informs us of who God is, but it transforms our spiritual lives, our words, and our deeds in our context (Yust, p. 10). If young men are to be ***transformed by faith***, they must move ***beyond affiliation*** with the faith community ***to a commitment*** of faith (Dean, p. 147).

E. ***Make young men "agents of mission."*** As mission agents, their identities and practices will be shaped to the church's mission. Transform young men by—
   1) Engaging them in "preaching" and teaching.
   2) Tithing.
   3) Giving sacrificial commitments.

4) Developing meaningful relationships with the needy.
5) Placing them in the leadership of the worshipping community (Dean, p. 148).

F. ***Develop "faith practices"*** to transform unfaithful young men into the faithful. Make it a practice to—
   1) Include them as ***"permanent partners in ministry."***
   2) Turn over the leadership to them in worship, hospitality, and service.
   3) Give them a ***sense of belonging*** to the faith community by integrating them into adult responsibility on a regular basis.
   4) Make them "insiders" who are passionate for the work of Christ (Dean, pp. 149, 150).

It is my hope that the above ***faith practices*** will transform young Black men by engaging them in positive relationships and care giving attitudes toward others.

Part 2: The Implicit Thesis: Why Shape Boys through a Rite of Passage?

The implicit thesis of this book is to determine whether a Pastor led, and church based Rite of Passage process, can intentionally help Black male boys transition into adulthood with a sense of self-identity, purpose, direction, and social responsibility. Can a program of this type serve as a deterrent to aggressive and negative social behavior of some adolescent males? Can a program of this type give adolescent boys a sense of pride, a place of belonging, encouragement, self-respect, recognition, discipline, leadership, and a spiritual foundation?

What is a rite of passage? A rite of passage is a way for an adolescent male to gain self-identity; it is a way to know when and where a transition into adulthood and social responsibility has taken place. Hare and Hare (1985), in Bringing the Black Boy to Manhood: The Passage, have noted that a rite of passage gives an adolescent boy a sense of becoming an adult, a sense of the sacredness of self, of purpose, responsibility, and manly commitment as a social being versus the sexual being.

In The Warrior Within, Moore & Gillette (1992) assert that a ***rite of passage*** allows a boy and man "to gain maturity and generativity, [where] he must accept his ***sword*** (***scepter*** – symbol of mature masculine life-force, Moore & Gillette, 1992, p. 152), make decisions, and take responsibility for planning and implementing effective action" (p. 153). The rite of passage moves the boy into the "drama of sacrifice" where he gives himself to a cause greater than himself. In the rite of passage, the boy is "reborn, and reinvested with the power of a higher good. Through masculine initiation, the *hero* becomes a *warrior* in the service of the King" [in the Christian understanding, King Jesus] (Moore & Gillette, 1992, p. 154).

The ***rite of passage*** gives an adolescent boy a social potency and relationship. The customs, rituals, and ceremonies gives to the adolescent a special quality, a purpose, function, and connectedness to the holy, the sacred, and the imperatives of that mystery (pp. 20-22).

> For females toward the end of latency, there is typically the crisis of menstruation and its physical sequelae to signal the indelible fact of womanhood and the woman's biosocial imperatives. For the male there is no corresponding biological jolt. His awareness of his puberty and his potentialities are more subtle and bound to the dictates of sexual pleasure as over against the sobering qualities of the female's concomitant pain and pregnability. Hence, societies historically have struggled through initiation rites and related feats, ordeals, scarification, and artificial traumas, to provide the boy with a psychosocial jolt into manhood (p. 18).

A. The Shaping of a Man Child: Nelson Mandela's Rite of Passage

In the book, Long Walk to Freedom, Nelson Mandela (1994) describes his rite of passage (related feats, ordeals, scarification) that jolted him into a psycho-social manhood of responsibility and respectability among his tribal community:

> When I was sixteen, the regent decided that it was time that I became a man. In the Xhosa tradition, this is achieved through one means only: circumcision. In my tradition, an uncircumcised male cannot be heir to his father's wealth, cannot marry or officiate in tribal rituals. An uncircumcised Xhosa man is...not considered a man at all, but a boy (p. 22).

For Mandela (1994) and the Xhosa people, circumcision meant the incorporation of the male into the society. It is a ritual from which a man dates his years. To enter into manhood, each initiate is enrolled in a circumcision school. One custom was to perform a daring exploit before the ceremony. The night before the ceremony the community would sing and dance. At dawn, the initiates would bathe in the river's cold waters, a ritual of purification. With the parents, relatives, chiefs, and counselors gathered, the ceremony would begin with drums pounding. The initiates would sit on blankets on the ground naked with their legs spread. The initiate was not to flinch or cry out for this would show weakness and stigmatized one's manhood.

Circumcision was a trial of bravery and stoicism. There was no anesthetic for a man was to suffer in silence. An *ingcibi,* a circumcision expert would kneel in front of each boy and with his *assegai* (circumcision knife) change boys to men in a single blow (Mandela, 1994). Mandela describes his rite of passage:

> I looked directly into his eyes. He was pale, and though the day was cold, his face was shining with perspiration. His hands moved so fast they seemed to be controlled by an otherworldly force. Without a word, he took my foreskin, pulled it forward, and then, in a single motion, brought down his assegai. I felt as if fire was shooting through my veins;...Many seconds seemed to pass before I remembered the cry...*Ndiyindoda!* (I am a man!) (p. 24).

As a result of the passage, Mandela said, "I might marry, set up my own home, and plow my own field. I could now be admitted to the councils of the community; my words would be taken seriously. At the ceremony, I was given my circumcision name, Dalibunga, meaning "Founder of the Bungha," the traditional ruling body of the Transkei...and I was proud to hear my new name pronounced: Dalibunga" (p. 24).

Many adolescent African American boys remain boys even in adulthood. Without a rite of passage ritual as a sign of transition from adolescence to adulthood many African American boys will continue to experience an "extended adolescence" (Hare and Hare, 1985) where they do not know who they are (self-identity) or what it means to be a responsible adult.

The African American adolescent lives in a context where he does not rule, but is basically under female rule in a single parent context. The adolescent male does not experience ruler(ship) in a church context because he is slow to volunteer for places of service or leadership. The adolescent male is not in a context where he is given responsibility. In many cases, his only leadership is seen in sports versus leadership in the academic or business fields. As a result, the African American adolescent male is mission(less) and irresponsible.

The task is to ask, how can African American adolescents discover who they are in God and thus what God has for their lives that they too might have dominion? How can the question be answered in their lives, "What is my life in an ultimate sense coming to? How will I make a significant difference?"

This rite of passage process should begin with 5 - 7 adolescent male participants ranging in ages from 13 to 18 years old. A projected time frame of 3 months (February - April 1996) is required. The group sessions will be designed as a series of passages through which I and the boys will enter and transcend. These stages (passages) of development should help the adolescent understand his identity in relation to others with the desired outcome of being seen as a significant and contributing member of the church congregation and the community as a whole, thus creating within them a positive esteem and image.

B. The Shaping of a Man Child Begins: The Rite of Passage Story

It was June of 1990. I had just resigned a full time teaching position of seven years at a Christian elementary school in Chicago, Illinois. I went from the school to assume a full time pastorate at the First Baptist Church, University Park, Illinois. As I sat in my small office trying to figure out what I would do next, the church doorbell rang. A woman and her teenage son were standing there. I invited them in and this mother began to pour out her frustration as it related to her 15 year old son's dilemma: "Pastor, I don't attend your church, but I need help with my boy. He was kicked out of the high school and was told not to come back. He won't listen to me; he disrespects me; he curses me out, and unless you can do something with him, I'm going to put him out!"

Following this incident, there paraded before me in the years that followed, cases of other adolescent males who found themselves in troubled and trying situations:

> A 15 year old was arrested and interrogated in a case of discharging an unregistered, sawed-off shotgun through a neighborhood window. In an outburst of denial, he yelled, "Pastor, I did not do it! I was framed by the guy who did it! Why did he lie on me?" Later, I stood speechless with him and his mother as he faced an uncertain future in a Will County courtroom. Thankfully, the charges were dropped. He was the wrong suspect.
>
> I sat silent with a grief stricken father as he and I peered through a glass shield at his 17 year old son who was awaiting trial in a murder case. He is now serving a 60 year sentence with hope of a new trial.
>
> Looking in the side window of a Cook County detective's police car, a 16 year old member of our church was arrested in an alleged gang drive by shooting.

> I stood looking down in the face of an 18 year old. He had been shot and left for dead in a suburban shopping mall. Peering at the tubes in his nose and stomach, I told him that I would do what I could to help him start over again. I wanted him to live out his days; I wanted him to become a man; I wanted him to carry on the name of his father who had died four years earlier whom I had loved very much as a friend.

As a result of these experiences, I asked, "Am I my brother's keeper?" Am I responsible for youth development into maturity? Upon reflection, I wondered how could I and the church help? How could adolescent males be directed toward growth? In speaking with our church's Youth Minister and Deacons' ministry leader, we discussed that there were few identified programs of initiation celebrations that marks a point whereby adolescent males can be said to have transitioned into adulthood. We concluded that without such programs, adolescent males would continue to be retarded in their maturation process.

To further explicate the social condition, Lee Butler (1997) in a sermon titled "Marked By Mercy" says—

> When we talk about what it means to be a man, we (African American men) are often forced to understand ourselves in the social context from a conspiracy model where we say "they" are out to get us or we view ourselves from a deficiency model that concludes "we" can go so far or high because of what we are made of.
>
> When men in the Black context are talked about by others, they are mentioned in the context of fratricide and genocide—"brothers killing brothers and everyone else."

> What makes the Black presence so different among others in the human family to the extent that Black men are classified as an "endangered species?" This is not said about all men, but about Black men.

The *specific problem in this practice of ministry* centers on how can a partnership of relationship be defined and adolescent maturation experienced? I believe that a Rite of Passage Program centered in a church context can educate, encourage, and reform the thinking of adolescent males who are in search for identity.

This project and process of partnership with adolescents is significant because it *attempts to encourage liberation among adolescent males.* I believe their liberation must be a freedom from what Turner (1995) calls "liminality" or "no place." The present social structure to which an adolescent grows puts him in a condition of negative transition to which he is not adequately equipped to handle, understand, or accept. For many African American males, adolescence becomes an involuntary transition from a meaningful position and place in the culture and community. In this ***liminal*** (in-between) period, there is confusion and ambiguity as it concerns their vocation for his future.

When an adolescent male attempts to find social acceptability outside of the adult world of rules and regulations, his efforts are interpreted as unacceptable behavior. This period of socially induced ***liminality*** (being separated and living betwixt and between social contact and relationship) is oppressive. It is a period of darkness where no one knows his name; he is invisible; he is "the problem"; he possesses nothing; he has no status, no property, no insignia, no rank, no role, or position along side of others. In this state, there is no one to show him the way because he is feared.

The adolescent male finds himself in a dialectical situation. He wants to affirm himself, but he is expected to behave passively, to obey implicitly, and accept punishment without complaint. The adolescent male is in the "in-between." As a result, the adolescent is "imageless," "personless," and his struggle is to be free; he wants to be "something" over against "nothing." The goal of the Rite of Passage is to bring the adolescent into community and social relationship (See Turner, 1995, pp. 94-96).

This Rite of Passage project is designed to encourage change in how adolescent males image themselves. Using insight from Cairns (1994), this project will attempt to become a laboratory of liberation for adolescent males in a context of mutuality. It will attempt to critically examine the issues that chain them in psychological and social bondage. The immersion of adolescent males into partnership with adult males is an initiatory event that will be dialogical in its process. It will attempt to be a process of mutual education where both adults and adolescents are taught by one another. The structure of this project will be that of a journey that is ever in process and change.

A Rite of Passage serves an adolescent male as a point of initiation and transition into adult responsibility. In my own experience, I cannot pinpoint a place of transitioning into adulthood. The process is noteworthy to help me identify key persons who helped me through this period of searching and significance.

Why is a Rite of Passage significant to the development of adolescent males? In his study on Manhood in the Making: Cultural Concepts of Masculinity, Gilmore (1990) notes that all societies offer a way of being an approved adult male. He says that each society has "manhood ideals" that psychologically integrate men into their community. In most instances, the "ideals of manhood" are put to the test in adolescent rite of passages. These are tests or indoctrinations that happen before the boys and youths are awarded their manhood.

Each society has an "image" of manhood that is problematic, but all have a "testing" that boys must pass through. These tests determine whether an adolescent will be labeled a weakling. He must demonstrate a "courageous action," be a warrior, be moral, a problem solver, and demonstrate a skill and endurance. To prove manhood, he must stand up to insults and be self-reliant. He must be serviceable to the community (Gilmore). The basic assumption in all societies is that "men are made, not born."

A Rite of Passage is important because it serves as a point where adolescent males can be identified as "initiated persons." It is needed because there is a crisis in adolescent male identity. Moore and Gillette (1990) have noted that the disappearance of the father through emotional or physical abandonment brings psychological devastation to the children—both male and female.

As it relates to the adolescent male, the ***absent father*** cripples the son's ability to gain a gender identity, and thus diminishes his ability to relate in intimate and positive ways with both males and females (Moore & Gillette, 1990). How is the father absent in our contemporary society? The ***absent father*** is unavailable by "emotional distance;" some are absent through "physical distance" because of their work; others are absent through divorce or separation; still others are absent through drug and alcohol use, thus robbing their children the blessedness of relatedness (Moore & Gillette, 1993, p. 108).

Adolescent boys need help in developing their potential. In the book, The Warrior Within, Moore & Gillette (1992) suggests a need to regain "legitimate masculine greatness" (p. 148). Men and boys need to be taught to be ***generative*** in the larger world. The challenge is to help boys develop their mission. Moore & Gillette (1992) states, "Men should be empowered. They need encouragement to accept, experience, and exercise their power. The initiatory processes…[is to help] teach men how to become responsible, nurturing, and powerful" (p. 150).

Boys need positive models of maleness to inspire them to leadership in society. In the absence of initiating men in society, boys do not mature. Without mentors to help guide boys into living productively, they will never learn nor exercise leadership in the home, workplace, or society (Moore & Gillette, 1993, pp 107 - 108).

A ***Rite of Passage*** takes into consideration the ritual processes of initiating adolescents into mature adult responsibility. Within our church community, at present, Boy Scouts offer an identifiable ritual process of initiating adolescent males into maturity and responsibility. Moore and Gillette (1990) note that many adolescents have been involved in no initiations or "pseudo-initiations" which have advanced and advocated a psychology of dominance (military boot camp, gangs, prisons run by gangs, drive by shootings). These pseudo-initiations have made it easy for adolescents to act out behaviors that are violent, hostile, and abusive against others. These pseudo rites have only perpetuated dominance, hindered creativity, and have left the adolescent at immature levels.

A Rite of Passage can be a positive "transformative initiatory process." It can be a step toward "rebirth." The Passage offers a death of the old self of the adolescent, with its negative attachments, and old ways of thinking, doing, and feeling. As a result of the process of initiation, a new being, a resurrected person submitted to God with compassion, and clarity of vision can emerge as a result of the ritual process. The Passage is an opportunity to help direct an adolescent's power into responsibility and spirituality. It can help bring a diffused adolescent identity into a structured one. The goal is to help adolescents transition into adulthood that is not clouded with dominance or (dis)empowering behavior toward others (Moore & Gillette, 1990).

In consultation with the parents, their concern centers on the above issues. As a pastor, my concern centers on adult men partnering with adolescents in co-learning situations that are meaningful, instructive, and ***liberative*** (freeing) to both parties involved.

The context of this Rite of Passage is limited to the First Baptist Church, University Park, Illinois. This church is a predominately African American congregation in a village comprised of about 6,200 residents - 79% African American and 19% Euro-American. The village has the land space to house 100,000 residents. It is located about 25 miles south of Chicago, Illinois. First Baptist Church of University Park is a church that has its membership from the surrounding townships of Crete, Park Forest, Matteson, Richton Park, Steger, and Country Club Hills. The largest attendance of the church's youth population is from University Park.

University Park contains no impoverished areas. Up scale housing is slowly being built in the village at an average cost of $95,000 to $129,000 dollars. It is not racially segregated. The existing housing is moderately priced including single family housing, condominiums and townhouse developments. The village is divided between apartment dwellers and home owners.

University Park is the home of Governors State University. It is a commuter college with an enrollment of approximately 6,000 students. The school district's educational system has been reorganized to accommodate a diverse student population. Five elementary schools have been classified as first through fourth grade centers. One fifth through sixth grade center has been established to bring children across the district together earlier in an integrative forum. This center houses all of the resources from across the district to facilitate excellence in education. The reconstruction of the middle school will bring all seventh through eighth graders across the district to University Park. The high school is located in Crete, Illinois. The racial make up of the student population of the middle school and high school are roughly 60% Euro-American and 40% African American.

University Park has six established congregations. First Baptist is the oldest of the churches being 36 years old. The church transitioned from Euro-American to African American in 1986.

C. The Purpose of the Man Child Project

The purpose of this project is the maturation and re-imaging of African American adolescent males. Many are voiceless and defined as the perpetrators of victimization. They are labeled as "trouble makers." They are classified as "hyperactive" and their addiction to drugs begins in school through medicating them to control them. They are called "predators." They are not taken seriously. They are not listened to; their creativity and their desire to be a part of a significant group is stifled. They are silenced in jails, juvenile detentions, school detentions, suspensions, and expulsions. At home they are given no meaningful responsibility. At church, they are not challenged. In society, they are the unemployed. To gain identity, they "hang" together and are eventually socialized and initiated into gang or destructive activity, never really growing up or moving to a stage of social responsibility and respect.

The basic assumption of this project is that adolescent males can be "free to be" through a cooperative team approach and partnership. Barbour et al (1994) suggests how the exploitation of adolescent males can be overcome through a plan of action and reflection. The action and reflection must –

1. be a shared responsibility between adults and the initiants;
2. be a genuine relationship of dialogue and mutuality must be established to give a voice to empower the locked out;
3. ask adults and adolescents to cross the boundary of their own experiences to bridge the gap to understand each other's culture;
4. each together must identify their goals;
5. each must be aware of how they oppress each other and change;
6. must have learning's that are shared tasks where both are open for questions in an involved manner; and

7. each must commit to contribute their talents and resources to the partnership of relationship without either being controlling.

What follows next is the journey toward maturation. I will attempt to describe the efforts made in this liberation partnership and the changes that occurred after reflection on the first Rite of Passage attempt in 1995-1996. In this second Rite of Passage, 1996-1997, I and others are attempting to move from an adult directed approach to a dialogical/partnership approach with the adolescent males. Mandela (1994), in his book <u>Long Walk To Freedom,</u> summarizes this task—

> I have walked that long road to freedom. I have tried not to falter; I have made missteps along the way. But I have discovered the secret that after climbing a great hill, one only finds that there are many more hills to climb. I have taken a moment here to rest, to steal a view of the glorious vista that surrounds me, to look back on the distance I have come. But I can rest only for a moment, for with freedom comes responsibilities, and I dare not linger, for my long walk is not yet ended (p. 544).

D. The Theory of the Rite of Passage Proposal

The aim of this Rite of Passage proposal is to encourage Black male initiants toward a new "self-consciousness" that is dialectically opposed to the social construct of nihilism. Second, it attempts to offer adults an opportunity to participate in adolescent actualization. The hope is that adults can serve as interpretive (hermeneutical) instruments to help Black males understand the history and present moral and psychological dilemma that affects their self understanding.

The basic theoretical assumption is that Black male adolescents and adults have been educated toward the denial of their essential selves and humanity. This denial of self has happened through a generational educative process that has lead to the present moral and psychological deformation of many adolescents. Because of the generational cycle of deformation many adolescent males grow up and begin to live frustrated and ashamed of their maleness. To reverse and counteract some of the above assumptions, I believe that a liberation model of education can begin to re-shape and regenerate the adolescent to a new "consciousness" of esteem, self-determination and development.

The theory used to inform this practice of ministry will be Freire's (1995) Pedagogy of the Oppressed. Are Black adolescent males oppressed within the African American context? Can a pedagogy of partnership with adolescent males make a difference in how they view and envision themselves? Freire's (1995) construction of partnership believes that the oppressed are awakened to their condition of helplessness when others challenge them to resist the forces that enslave them.

This partnership is located and limited to a church setting because of the easy access to the adolescents, parents, and other concerned adults. The goal is to expand this model into the community with the church being the center for spiritual direction to support both males and females who struggle with identity formation. This program should include adolescent initiants from ages 11 to 18 years of age.

The key element in Freire's (1995) ***educational liberation partnership*** is its humanizing quality that is akin to the Christian faith. Freire (1995) believes that both humanization and dehumanization are possibilities inherent in the experience of each individual. There is sin in all of us, and hope for the worst of us. We allow ourselves to be dehumanized because we lack a "consciousness" about our possibility toward beauty, maturity, creativity, and the **generativity** of humanity.

Freire (1995) believes at the heart of each individual is the yearning to recover their lost humanity. To "partner" with oppressed adolescents is to help them become aware and break free of the structures that maintain their oppression and immaturity. ***A pedagogy of partnership*** should help reshape and re-socialize adolescents from a destructive ethos of life. The partnership should give to adolescents a new interpretive framework where they gain a sense of self-worth, and dignity.

To help Black male adolescents move toward maturity, their oppressed "consciousness" must be reshaped and changed. A pedagogy of partnership can encourage a matured adolescent consciousness that should lead to transformed behavior. A pedagogy of partnership should allow adults to ***stand as partners*** with adolescents in a ***praxis of humanization***.

Black men can help Black boys ***reflect and dialogue*** about their particular socialization and make plans and actions to transform it. Freire (1995) affirms that a ***praxis and strategy for humanization must be developed by the oppressed; therefore this strategy must be developed by the adolescent.*** The challenge of partnership should allow adolescent males the opportunity to develop their strategy to creatively address the powers that hinder their growth and maturation.

Freire (1995) further suggests that ***a liberation consciousness*** comes through an educational process. He notes that the ***"banking"*** model of education is ineffective to create a liberated person. It is not transformative, but compartmentalized. The *banking model* limits creativity in the learner. There is manipulation and not a relationship between the teacher and student.

The ***revolutionary model*** that Freire (1995) presents brings the student and the teacher into partnership. The concept of ***paternalism*** is rejected. The learner is challenged to become creative, mature, and responsible. Learning is done through common reflection where both teacher and student are re-creators and learners.

A Rite of passage, as ***partnership education,*** stresses that a "consciousness of humanization" is done through "problem posing education." Problem posing education embodies communication, dialogical relationships, cooperation, and critical reflection between ***students and teachers***. In this method, ***no one teaches another, but each teaches the other.*** There is reciprocal learning and teaching. There is real dialogue in the light of each others reflections. According to Freire (1995), this approach will lead the learner to feel free to pose questions and challenge problems related to their world. This challenge to interrelate to problems in context will evoke from adolescents new understandings and will gradually lead them to becoming committed to overcoming the practices of domination within themselves and others around them.

E. The Shaping of the Rite of a Passage Project

With the above considerations in mind, the vision is to partner together both the Black male child/youth and adult to encourage a relationship of mature adult development. The questions to be considered are, "In what ways can adolescent males be transformed from society's deformation? How can the pastor and the church's adult male constituency encourage the Black child to reflect and pattern an image of mature adult responsibility?"

The biblical task is to bring the Black male child into the consciousness that they are "representatives of God." Based on the biblical relationship of *Adam* with God, these initiants should know that they too have a ***"graced partnership"*** with God that declares that their life is sacred to God and that God is imminently present to them.

The pedagogy of partnership should reflect on the initiant's **sense of *mission***. In Genesis 1:26 is the word "dominion." *Adam* was given a mission of dominion, not domination. His dominion was a responsibility of leadership over the earth. This mission of responsibility suggests that ***God expects young men to do something*** with their lives in the context of creation.

To help young men recognize their self-image as relational beings, it is necessary to develop a context where they can share with others. Many male adolescents experience isolation or exclusion instead of love. If they are to be transformed, then there must be an encounter of significant "love" with persons with whom they can identify.

The idea of partnership is significant for adolescent maturity because it affirms their dependence on and support from others as essential to life. They can see themselves as persons to whom others must put their trust. According to Bonhoeffer (1959), the idea of "partnership" is seen in the image of God which is an image of reflective and representative image of sociality and love.

God is a social reality and humanity is created in that image. God does not "make" and shape *Adam* alone. Many personalities are involved in the shaping of Adam. According to Genesis 1:26, others are involved in the shaping of *Adam*—whether the Spirit, the earth, the heavenly host, or the deliberation or sociality (Father, Son, Spirit) of God. In "Made in God's Image," Waters (1993) asserts that the image of God is a social reality. "The creation of humanity was the work of a social being. It is no wonder, then, that we are also social beings. We are meant to dwell together in community. We are meant to dwell together in relationship to one another" (p. 23).

1. Beginning the Rite of Passage Project

The ***Rite of Passage*** offers an opportunity for adults to partner with adolescent initiants in "a relationship of love." The following narration is the chronological process that was taken by myself and other adult partners to make "initiated men."

In November of 1995, five men gathered to discuss the possibility of developing a Rite of Passage Program. It was decided that I would be the chief guide or "ritual elder" of the project bringing to it scope and focus. The men agreed to serve as a "Council of Elders." Their task was to advise me on strategy for the program, as well as evaluate its progress, and serve as partners and sponsors to the initiants in the program.

2. The Structure of the Program

The first serious concern was the structure of the program. It was believed that these adolescents "had to go through something" to demonstrate they understood what it meant to be a man. The question arosc, what would be the challenges or passages, the initiants would have to go through to be considered "initiated men?" After deliberation, we figured seven passages should be encountered for a duration of six months culminating with a graduation in June on Father's Day.

The process was as follows—each initiant would meet with the pastor, as a group, for biblical foundations of the program. It was suggested that they should have a basic background in the poetry and literature of African Americans to give them a sense of historical continuity with their past. To give them contextual experience, each initiant was to have a session with adult males of the congregation who would share their story of transition from adolescence to adult responsibility.

I recommended that the initiants should understand basic adolescent psychology. The purpose was to give them a clue into their social behavior among their peers and other adults. Each adolescent was to have a session of interchange with his parents. The purpose was to establish a contract of responsibility within the home setting where they could demonstrate responsibility and maturation. Within the social environment, each adolescent was to do a school and church project that involved them working with their peers. The project was to be of their own choosing and design. Toward the end of the program, we decided that each initiant should be partnered with an adult male and taken on the job with them. This job partnership was to allow the initiants to see and experience what it meant to be involved in a day of work. The final phase was for the adolescents to attend a worship service with their parents and friends and be declared "initiated men." Each session and meeting would last for two and a half hours.

A. *The pastoral passage*

This passage was an intensive encounter with the pastor on issues that surrounded biblical foundations for leadership and faith development. I meet with the initiants for ***four consecutive sessions/weeks*** simply because that was the time it took to complete the assigned reading and discussion. It was decided that each passage would run as long as it took to finish it. As a result, the participation and the study were open as long as questions were asked. We discussed how people as David, Elisha, Timothy, and other biblical persons were in partnership with adults who helped them grow in the faith. As pastor, I was the ritual elder for each session. I designed and followed the initiants throughout the entire program.

The positive this passage offered was the presence of the pastor among the initiants. I believe my personal involvement with them demonstrated concern as well as a model of adult responsibility. The initiants gained a biblical reference for adult responsibility. They participated well in the discussions and were able to relate to the fact that God wanted to use them in achieving "mighty acts." The major set back was my not partnering with another adult person who would assist, learn, and take ownership and leadership of this passage with another group. The key is to find a person who has a passion for adolescents and can in fact become a ritual elder of a similar program.

B. The patri passage

This passage was designed with the idea of engaging the adolescents in conversation with mature adult men in the congregation. This was a ***one session/week*** experience. The term patriarch (father) was not meant to carry with it the negatives associated with historical patriarchy as a dominant male mindset (See Moore & Gillette 1990 on patriarchy), but it was meant to be a teaming of the adolescents with mature adult men (fathers) who would share their story of transition from adolescence to adult responsibility. The initiants had an opportunity to listen to the successes and failures of men in the congregation.

This session proved to be enlightening. Seven men shared their story and told of their adolescent struggles and the persons who were instrumental in guiding and inspiring them. The one missing element was the initiants response. We did not break down into small groups to ask the initiants to share their journey. I believe it would have been important to have allowed them to "map" their journey on newsprint as a visual means to discuss where they came from and to plot their future. One addition is to expand the sessions to include a "mapping" session for the initiants to help them see the direction God may be calling them. A correction that was suggested was to change the name of the passage to Ancestral Passage. This title suggests more of a spiritual African connection over against a hierarchical relationship.

C. The poetic passage

This passage was a journey through African American literature. The passage included ***four sessions/weeks*** of study. The positives of this passage was the introduction of liberation and accommodation poets in the 1920s, 1950s and the 1970s. As the ritual leader, I chose the poetry I felt would help identify the African American struggle for identity and liberation in those periods. The discussions and interpretation of the poetry and literature was astounding. The initiants demonstrated great insight and they were excited at each discussion.

At the final session, they were asked to write a poem that reflected their identity and struggle for liberation. During a Sunday morning worship, three of the initiants read their works. It was a moving part of the worship.

One of the draw backs that I perceived was my inability to allow the initiants to suggest poetry and literature of African American origin that they felt would be worthy of discussion. In a sense, I forced on them my favorite writers, not asking if there were persons they considered significant. To correct this oversight, in the second Rite of Passage, the initiants will be asked to chose a monthly reading from African American autobiographies or writings by authors of African origin. The initiants will be free to chose their readings and to share insights gained at following meetings on a monthly basis.

D. *The parental passage*

The parental passage was a self-directed initiative where the initiants were asked to interview their parents with a hope of gaining insight into their past, their history, and hopefully, their identity. The introductory session with the pastor was ***two sessions***. The first session was the explanation with the parents on what was expected. The second session was the group discussion of the progress made by the initiants.

The session with the parent was to last ***eight weeks*** leading up to the June ceremony and run concurrently with what we were doing in the large group sessions weekly in other passages. To my surprise, this experience was not taken seriously. They were to tape the conversation with their parents, and ask appropriate questions to come to an understanding of their identity. From the group discussions that followed the exercise, only a few seemed to appreciate knowing something about where they came from and the struggles their parents encountered. One other disappointment for me was that the initiants who had fathers did not interview them. The reasons given were they felt they could talk to their mothers more freely than their fathers.

To better enhance this session, I believe as a group, the initiants should formulate questions that they would be interested in asking their parents during the interview. I would also discuss beforehand reasons why interviewing the father is important to their identity as males.

The second aspect of this passage included home responsibilities. The initiants were to contract with their parents on responsibilities they would carry out for the duration of the program. There were weekly reports on this progress and the parents acknowledged a greater sense of responsiveness by the initiants.

E. The peer passage

This passage was to be an act of leadership carried out in the school and church context. There were ***two initial sessions*** where the goals and objectives of the project were to be considered. This passage was to run concurrently with our weekly meeting for ***twelve weeks*** to the end of school. In the school context, I visited the principals of the initiants and talked with them about the vision of the initiants taking leadership in the school. The principal, myself, and the initiants discussed possible options in the school that could serve as peer initiatives for them.

One advantage of this interview with the principal and the initiants was that it gave them a respectability in the administration's eyes. It offered them a one-on-one interview with the principal that was not in a conflict situation. Some of them served on the school's conflict management team and others got into service organizations for the year. One needed aspect of this passage is to build in a system of reporting on the school peer leadership project. The one drawback to this passage was the time it was initiated. It was started too late in the year. To be effective, this peer project should start at the beginning of the school session in September.

The church project was under the supervision of our church's minister of youth. There was ***one session*** whereby the goals and objectives were discussed. Each initiant was to serve as a youth advisor to our church's ministry base—Brotherhood, Singles Ministry, Sunday School, etc.

The initiants were put into service with the children's ministry and senior adult ministry. They were asked to serve on Sunday in the preschool and nursery division. Also, they helped in clean up and fix up projects around the church. The response of the initiants were positive. They said they felt accepted working with adult leadership groups. They shared that the opinions they offered to the church leadership appeared to be appreciated. The challenge now is to maintain their participation and input on an ongoing basis. The critique of this passage is the same as the peer passage, it should have started at the beginning of the program in September instead of toward the end; this would have allowed for a more effective follow up and evaluation of the initiant's progress.

F. The psychological passage

In this passage, I attempted to introduce the initiants to developmental theories that would help them understand their identity formation process. This passage lasted for ***three sessions***. I took excerpts from West (1994) and Thomas' (1993) study of systemic racism to help them understand their social self-understanding from a negative history that still influences their thinking and identity. We looked at

Erik Erikson's (1983) concept of adolescent "identity crisis and confusion."

We examined Janet Hale-Benson's (1982) theory of learning styles from a relational model. The discussions centered on interactive learning versus logical-mathematical learning. The draw back of this psychological passage was my inability to simplify it. I believe a better approach would have been to utilize actual learning experiences of the adolescents. The sessions and the theories presented appeared helpful to the adults who had adolescents at home. They asked the questions that related to adult and adolescent communication and relationship problems.

The major contribution the initiants brought to this passage was their rebuttals to adult observations of adolescent development and behavior. The interaction, though heated at times, gave the initiants opportunity for verbal expression. They were never told they were wrong, but they were encouraged to look at other options. We used hypothetical situations and asked them to discuss how they would solve the problem at hand. The key phrase the initiants used during the discussion was—"But you don't understand." After reflecting on the way I was raised, and the modern context they are encountering, I concluded that I did not understand.

G. The partnership passage

It was determined that one aspect of adult responsibility was the world of work. This passage lasted for ***three sessions***. We had the initial meeting with the adult men who would work with the initiants. The information that was shared centered around "the psychology of work." The initiants were asked to develop objectives that would help them transition into the world of work. In the group setting, these objectives were discussed. Upon asking them what their career goals were, we attempted to find persons in the congregation who were in those fields. The initiants were to involve themselves in conversation with these adults to get an idea of the challenges and preparations they would need for their career goals.

After these sessions, the initiants were partnered with men in the program who could take them on the job. Following the day on the job, the group shared their experiences. Each encounter proved beneficial. One of the initiants was offered a summer job. He worked that summer and upon entering college that fall was told he had a job each summer until graduation, and a permanent position after graduation, if this was his career choice.

In follow up with the men who served as partners, it was suggested that the partnership/work passage be placed at the beginning of the program in September. This shift would allow the initiants to encounter a number of job sights and experiences.

The challenge of this passage is to develop a process whereby the initiants continue working with their partners through high school, college or vocational years. One goal is to find partners whose jobs will establish intern programs and scholarships for these initiants who would be interested in that particular field of work.

H. The power passage

1. Aggressive Power

In childhood and adolescence, we see the rise of aggressive power in boys more readily in its outward expressions of "playing rough," "violent behavior," or "misbehavior." The challenge of the rite of passage is to ask how can "aggressive power" be used in the service of others to empower life and benefit others? How can aggressive power be mobilized in young men to meet life head on? How can aggressive power be used to help young men be assertive about their lives, goals, needs, and causes? (Moore & Gillette, 1992, pp. 98, 100, 101).

The true nature of men is assertiveness and affirmation. Men are needed to help boys know that assertiveness and affirmation are a part of their male powers. The challenge is how to lead boys from regressing into "child passivity" by dominating personalities (Moore & Gillette, 1992, pp. 102-103). In our culture, Black male aggression and assertiveness has been handled by imprisoning Black men, and "social engineering" of allowing boys to express only "so called feminine virtues" and not their masculine virtues. To keep boys docile, in this generation, there has been a "drug regimen to inhibit aggression" (Moore & Gillette, 1992, pp. 48-49).

Into Life: Read Mark 5:1ff. Discuss what the people did with a man that was aggressive. __________

____

What must men do with aggressive and assertive boys? Men must help boys learn how to 1) control aggression. 2) Men must help boys know when aggressiveness is called for. 3) Men must teach boys when to actualize ***useful aggression***. ***Useful aggression*** does the following (Moore & Gillette, 1992, pp. 104-105):

a. Seeks to make places safe.
b. In dangerous situations, it contributes to the welfare of the community.
c. It stops the bully who attacks and even if beaten we experience our power to respond to threatening situations, building courage and self-confidence.

Men must teach boys to use aggressive skills 1) to respond to problems that need to be attacked, 2) to face situations that need to be confronted, 3) to challenge dominating situations that browbeat, ridicule, and dominate our wives, children, families, and ourselves (Moore & Gillette, 1992, p. 105). Men are to teach boys to use aggressive power for good. Moore & Gillette (1992) affirm that aggressive power, in boys who will be men, is needed to face—

> Crippling and killing diseases, natural disasters, environmental decay, the catastrophic troubles of our

> inner cities, corrupt social and political systems, injustice in the workplace, all call for an aggressive response from human beings willing to be warriors. The oppression of one class by another, of one race, one sex, one religion, one nation by another: These things too require a compelling reaction. (p. 105).

Black men are called to teach Black boys what to be angry and aggressive about. The following story is told by a Jewish rabbi – "My son, God made anger for a purpose./ Only be careful how you spend your anger. There are many things we should not be angry about. We should save our anger for those things which demand it" (Moore & Gillette, 1992, p. 106).

2. Heroic Power

Every boy wants to be a hero and every man who did not do something heroic carries within his psyche a "hero desire" and a "hero mind." Heroic power must be mentored. Heroes help bring out the potential in others. A rite of passage program is needed to offer models of inspired leadership in our society.

The Black man must be the hero and the "father" to inspire young men to create something new, useful and beautiful (Moore & Gillette, 1992, p. 106). Black men must provide the vision for boys to gain the courage to stand up against obstacles, fear, depression, and despair to live and to flourish. This leadership must give boys determination, courage, and self-discipline (Moore & Gillette, 1992, p. 107).

In this study, young men have been carried through a series of ordeals and challenges to prepare them to be heroic. The goal is not to make them "cape crusaders" as Batman and Robin nor is it to make them "Supermen" who retreat to their crystal ice fortresses for reflection. The journey into adult responsibility is one that leads young men to "be something" and "do something." A hero is a person that "does something" to better the community and the family to which s/he are a part.

Who can be a hero? A ***hero*** is not a super star athlete or a pop star with money and a big name. A hero is a person who will love, sacrifice, and give what she or he has to better the family, the church, the community, and the world. A hero is a life-giver who gives sacrificially to build a better world.

In most traditional literature, a hero has been simply understood as a "warrior," a "knight," a "soldier," a person who seeks to transform the world for the good. Joseph Campbell (1949), in his book, <u>The Hero with a Thousand Faces</u> offers the following definitions of a hero from religious literature around the world. A hero is one who brings light, understanding, and enlightenment to the mind and soul (p. 388). A hero is one who will not turn back regardless of the difficulty of the task. The hero brings a revolution of spiritual significance to life. The hero brings maturity to the human condition (Campbell, 1949, p. 388).

The hero, according to Campbell, ***overcomes self-interests to revitalize the world***. A hero "faces…the dragon-terrors," and the "tyrant-monsters (Campbell,

1949, p. 10). The hero submits to a difficult task for others (Campbell, p. 16). The hero is limited, but battles past limitations to inspire others (Campbell, p. 19-20). The hero goes into the world to transform it (Campbell, p. 38) by attempting through warrior power to solve problems by waging war on sin, evil, and the devil with a hope of eliminating them (Carol Pearson, 1989, p. 77) and to overcome those who oppress the world (Campbell, p. 29). The hero makes the world a sanctified and holy place by their efforts to bring life and renewal to it (Campbell, p. 43).

In her book, The Hero Within, Carol Pearson (1989) takes the idea of the hero beyond "the heroic ideal" of the warrior, being only a white man rescuing the damsel-in-distress or other ethnic men being sidekicks. None of us are sidekicks because the heroic nature is in each of us and challenges us to go on our journeys and claim our heroism, and make an essential contribution to the world. The hero, for Pearson, is one who wants to go deeper, being authentic, and empowered (Pearson, 1989, p. 2, xv). Each person has "a heroic consciousness" of optimism and possibility (Pearson, 1989, p. xix). The hero, in all of us, desires to confront the "dragons," the powers of non-life, to bring life and change to our culture and world. To not take the risk and the journey beyond our prescribed roles is to feel empty and discouraged (Pearson, 1989, p. 1).

An expanded definition of the hero is the person who is a responsible (Pearson, p. 45) and a responsive person. The hero takes responsibility for their personal lives and the lives of others. The hero places him/herself in situations where people are threatened, troubled, and needs help, and acts to change their lives. The hero ***helps us get "unstuck"*** and enables us to go on with our lives (Pearson, pp. 44, 42, & 150). The hero helps us get through our ***"crisis** (moments when we lose control of the fabric of our lives)* ***and trauma*** *(those gut-wrenching and mind-bending life changes)"* (Moore & Gillette, 1993, pp. 117, 119, 120, & 121) and dark moments of our experience. They move us into "sacred time and space" that gives us a more "mature way of being human" (Moore & Gillette, 1993, p. 107).

A hero is one who gets him or herself ***"unstuck"*** from his or her own difficult experiences of powerlessness, pain, loneliness, fear (Pearson, p. 82) and ***"crazy times."*** The "crazy times" are the periods of uncertainty where assumptions are stripped away one by one (Moore & Gillette, 1993, pp. 110, 119; For an example of crazy times see pp. 122 & 124). Once "unstuck," from the "crazy times" and "crisis" of one's own experience, the hero goes on a journey of getting others "unstuck" and released from their "crazy times," and "crisis" converting, transforming, and making the world a better place (Pearson, p. 83). The hero's task is to move beyond "slaying" or "converting" dragons. The hero becomes a "bridge" that leads people to grow through debate, brainstorming, sharing, dialogue, and exchange of ideas "to enlighten the world" and to "affirm the deepest level of truth about it" (Pearson, pp. 90, 91, 125). The new hero attempts to lead everyone to growth.

> [The] hero moves from warrioring into a more generative mode and devotes his [her] life to caring…supporting./ [L]earing to nurture and care for and, in doing so, gaining an identity that is less confined by the culture's more stereotyped images of masculinity makes it possible to move on to more complex ways of warrioring" (Pearson, p. 94).

The hero who continues to live a life of "struggle against others" or the powers of evil will ***"burn out"*** or become critically wounded by the forces they fight. Some who fight have become addicted to caffeine, uppers, and/or alcohol to keep going onward and upward" (Pearson, p. 96). The true hero moves "beyond the one up/one down view of life" (Pearson, p. 96) to "influencing" the world and extending their arms to honor and love themselves and others (Pearson, p. 97).

The hero is a person of "***transformative sacrifice"*** who gives themselves up and takes responsibility and responds to real needs in specific situations. The hero will endure hardship to care for others and spend their entire lives helping, committing to other persons, and causes (Pearson, pp. 111, 105, 104, 103, & 109).

The hero's ***life is a contribution*** to be given freely (Pearson, p. 115). The reward of the hero is 1) knowing that their lives have brought transformation and new life (Pearson, p. 115 & 152). The hero knows he or she will receive what they need to continue to give lovingly to life.

I. The processional passage

The final phase of the shaping of a vital man child is the graduation and induction ceremony. This ceremony can be conducted on Father's Day in June or during the Sunday morning worship of the group's chosing. The initiants, their parents, friends, teachers, the Council of Elders, and congregation should celebrate and mark this as a point of transition into being considered "initiated men."

After the ceremony, the initiants are to take their place in and among the socially responsible (See Appendix E).

3. The Re-Design of the Project: The Second Attempt

As a result of the foregone discussion, it is believed that a Rite of Passage approach is a proper tool to encourage adolescent maturation into adult responsibility. The program in its first administration in 1995 was designed to meet on a weekly basis. It was determined that this process was too rigid and too much like a school model. It was redesigned with four essential meetings in September, the first being with the parents and initiants, and the final three being with the initiants and the pastor. The group would meet thereafter once a month for reflection and discussion through June.

After evaluation of the first Rite of Passage, it was determined that the learning process should be more visual to coincide with the youth visual culture. We began to use more videos and newspaper cartoons that had religious, social, and cultural suggestions to enhance the learning process. The one advantage of this approach was that it was entertaining and fun. After the visuals, a discussion would follow with each person sharing insight as to how the video or cartoon related to their experience and the experience of other adolescents with whom they associated.

To understand the Rite of Passage process, we watched "Roots: The Video," Volume I. The section of interest centered around Kunta Kente's Rite of Passage process. We noted that his father taught him to learn by giving him responsibilities. This was significant to his esteem building. The mother and the grandmother played significant parts in his maturation process as advisors.

In the opening sessions and throughout the second Rite of Passage program, we had a grandmother and two mothers sit in on several sessions. These mothers – one single, one married – appreciated the opportunity to hear some things as it related to responsibility and male identity. During a number of sessions, both mothers contributed to the discussion and offered insight into the woman's role in adolescent male development.

To further explicate the analysis of this project, I would like to look at the culture, tradition, and theological basis used to analyze the effectiveness of this Rite of Passage strategy.

A. The Context

Using Killen & de Beer's (1995) The Art of Theological Reflection and Whitehead & Whitehead's (1995) Method in Ministry, I was able to examine the "experience" aspect of the adolescents. These authors hold experience as key to reflection and insight. These methods encouraged me to ask, "What experiences can be used to encourage the initiants to re-examine their feelings of low esteem and negative self concept?" "How can the negative indoctrination that has systemically worked against esteem building and identity formation be transformed to encourage adolescent males toward actualization and humanization?"

The issue of success for a project of this kind centers on the relationship between the number of single parent homes versus two parent homes, versus those in foster care; the number of "at risk" youth—those in the Department of Children and Family Services, the Juvenile Court system, those arrested by police, in jail, and those suspended from school, the number of drop outs as a result of school failure, and those males diagnosed with Attention Deficit Disorder.

In the course of the writing of this paper, one of the adolescents, a tenth grader, was arrested on school grounds for disorderly conduct. He was expelled from the high school for two years. In order to return, he was required to do forty hours of community service and demonstrate a changed attitude within that two year period. He has been enrolled in another school district and is presently seeking to fulfill the responsibilities needed to restore his name and reputation at his previous school. Using the method of reflection upon one's experience, we are having the initiant ask questions of what he could have done differently in that context, and when faced with another situation of similar magnitude, what will be his course of action? I believe this process has helped him to accept his present state of affairs, and has encouraged him to realize that he is not a failure, but a person of worth who made a mistake and has the power to start again.

B. An Exploration Pedagogy

To establish a pedagogy *(a pedagogy is a way or method of teaching children and youth)* that attempts to lead adolescent into insight concerning service, self-identity, esteem, mission, and maturation, Killen & de Beer's (1995) concept of ***"exploration"*** is a way to give the adolescents "ownership." ***Ownership*** was enhanced through the adolescents' envisioning what the Rite of Passage program's structure could be for them. Each initiant was asked to share "experiences, feelings, images, and insights" that were significant to them. It was hoped that their "personal experience" with adults in various contexts would lead them to "insight" and "action" concerning their responsibility in the society.

As a result of this "process of exploration," and my reflection on the initial program, the rite of passage will be restructured to incorporate the following aspects as tools for interpretation—experience, feelings, images, insight, and action. Example:

Pastoral Passage—Objectives:

a) Share biblical basis for transitioning from adolescence to adult responsibility.
b) Describe healthy esteem from a biblical perspective. Describe, write, or draw feelings, images, insights, and actions that resulted from this encounter.

Partnership Passage—Objectives:

a) Develop objectives that includes educational and vocational goals.
b) Partner youth with adult sponsors for counsel, encouragement, and evaluation.
c) Experience a day on the job with an adult partner. Have adult men share their experience of transitioning from adolescence to adult responsibility. Discuss the psychology of work.
d) Describe, write, or draw feelings, images, insights, and actions that resulted from this encounter.

Poetic/Ancestral Passage. Objectives:

a) Study contemporary and historical writers within the African American context.

b) Encourage creativity and interpretive skills.
c) Discover the prophetic voice of the past and present.
d) Write, draw feelings, images, insights, and actions that resulted from this encounter.

Parental Passage—Objectives:

a) Involve youth intentionally in dialog with their parents concerning their ancestors—grandparents, uncles, etc.
b) Interview parents concerning their history—childhood, youth, young adult.
c) Correlate and contrast their history with your self-identity. Describe, write, or draw feelings, images, insights, and actions that resulted from this encounter.

Peer Passage—Objectives:

a) Develop a group project within the church and community.
b) Develop an individual project in your school. Describe, write, or draw feelings, images, insights, and actions that resulted from this encounter.

C. The Tradition

In the African American religious context, the church building is a symbol of ownership. The initiants "own" and are "owned" figuratively by the church. The church building offers symbols of the faith to encourage faith development. The church building offers a space that is sacred and is a space that is literally "safe" from the "troubles of this world."

The pastor is a symbol of moral leadership and responsibility. My engagement with the initiants attempted to stimulate a sense of mission, purpose, and responsibility. It is hoped that this position of spiritual authority encouraged them toward esteem and self-concept development.

The key biblical text used to help encourage spiritual maturation was Genesis 1:26 (NRSV)—"Let us make *humankind* in our own image." This scripture centered on Adam's place, responsibility, and leadership in the context of creation. Other biblical texts used to encourage adolescent maturation are Prov. 22:6 (NRSV)—"Train children in the right way, and when old, they will not stray." Prov. 3:1 (NRSV)—"My child, do not forget my teaching, but let your heart keep my commandments." Deut. 6:6ff (NRSV), "Keep these words that I am commanding you today in your heart./ Recite them to your children and talk about them when you are at home and when you are away…" Eph. 6:4 (NRSV)—"And, fathers, do not provoke your children to anger, but bring them up in the discipline and instruction of the Lord." Reflections are to be made on these passages and others that are significant in developing a foundation for adolescent maturation.

D. The Culture

To examine the issues related to adolescent identity development, I examined the work of Eybers (1991) Pastoral Care to Black South Africans. Using Erikson's theory of adolescent identity and role confusion, he examines why adults do not take responsibility in building self-concept and identity in their youth. He based this theory on a generational cycle of failure that is passed from one generation to the next. To combat this cycle, he suggests a hermeneutic of interpretation to give adolescence a way to understand who they are in their social context.

Janice Hale-Benson (1992) has been useful in her critique of "Theories of Black Culture." She points to the period in schooling where adolescent males are considered a threat along with a shift in learning style that is not consistent with African American learning. She questions theories that attempt to minimize the values of the Black culture as not being viable and relevant to the development of its children and all children.

Other cultural texts used to encourage esteem, identity, and service—Nelson Mandela, Long Walk to Freedom, Alex Haley, Roots, Nathan McCall, Make Me Wanna Holler and poets as Hughes, Dunbar, MacKay, and Brown. These voices give clarity to the pain of self-denigration and the movement toward self-affirmation. The theological voices of the culture are explored by West (1994) and Thomas (1993) who reveal the systemic problems adolescents and adults face as a result of a racist culture. West (1994) offers a plan of "action" to combat the denigration of the self and its identity through moral action and initiative. Thomas (1993) examines the historical legacy of racism and why those structures of power still affect us today. These studies are significant in that they give adolescents the knowledge that they are not "the problem," but can be a part of the solution that struggles for justice and self-actualization.

E. Operational Theory

The operational theory of this project is based on an ***educational liberation model.*** It is believed that poor self-concept and low esteem are learned through a "banking system" that perpetuates an "I-It" or "Subject-Object" relationship among its teachers and learners. This system comprises, in part, negative unconscious parental actions, and/or intentional or unintentional strategies of educational institutions. The church has been a culprit in shaping the attitude of adolescent males in non-positive ways. My basic belief is that poor self-concept can be untaught when actions, projects, and partnerships with adolescents lead directly toward liberation and mission.

F. Actions: Becoming Men of Power

The above experiences and conversations with those in the first phase of this project has led me to the following conclusions for future work in this area of male maturation.

One of the major areas of concern as it relates to the ***educational liberation model*** is that of ***"enabling education"*** (Hooks, 1994). One of the temptations I faced as a leader in the rite of passage was to reinforce domination over the adolescents. I was in fact the authority and found myself limiting their freedom to be expressive in my desire to control the flow and outcome of the conversations. I still wanted to deposit things in them that I felt was good for them without allowing them to deposit who they were in me and each other.

In the attempt to make the rite of passage more "liberatory" and "empowering," I am attempting to use the suggestions of Hooks (1994) who believes that the learning and growing process can be liberating and enabling if it is exciting. The idea of excitement is a key concept. After reading Hooks (1994), I came to see that participation in the program was enhanced when excitement and fun were a part of the pedagogical process.

Putting excitement in the rite of passage was difficult for me because I did not know how to incorporate fun into our activities with the adolescents. Hooks (1994) has helped me in the process of understanding excitement when she says, "To encourage excitement [is] to transgress, [but] excitement [can] not be generated without a full recognition of the fact that there could never be an absolute set agenda governing teaching practices…be flexible…to allow for spontaneous shifts in direction… and interact according to their needs" (p. 7).

From Hooks' (1994) observation of learning as ***"enabling empowerment,"*** I have added to this ***pedagogy of partnership*** the idea that the passage should 1) be both exciting and pleasurable, 2) include dialogue with the adolescents that is open and flexible to shifts in direction to interact with needs versus the agenda, 3) generate excitement by demonstrating interest in the adolescents by hearing their voice and acknowledging them as persons of significant worth, 4) let them know that they are valued, 5) make them aware of their influence and contributions to the maturation process of others who are on the journey with them, 6) make them aware that "boys are made into men" through the collective efforts of the entire community, and 7) help them after their reflection on issues to take the actions necessary to change their world or situation to help them become self-actualized.

Hooks has challenged me to understand that maturation comes through a deliberate act of the adult partner engaging the adolescent to consider the issues they face that keeps them from being made whole. The adult partner must become what Hooks calls "a healer." As a healer, the adult partner helps the adolescent through periods of hostility, dysfunctional behavior, fear, and wounded psyches to a reality of wholeness where they are free to express themselves, share, and take risks in being open to and with others.

The adolescent must be challenged to become an active participant versus a passive recipient. For the adolescent to mature, the learning and activity environment must become dynamic. The adolescent must be encouraged to have an engaged voice that is ever in dialogue with diverse audiences of different opinions and ideas.

G. Evaluation

I offer the following insights to enhance the significance of the program.

a) See the project as a way of encouraging adolescent maturation into service and leadership functions.
b) Give ownership to the congregation through input, prayers, and partnership.
c) Give ownership to parents as partners in setting goals and commitment to their son's success in the project.
d) Establish guidelines in cooperation with each initiant who enters the project.
e) Discuss whether the mission and vision of the church correlates with a mission and vision of the initiants.
f) Move from a school "banking concept" of knowledge to "project orientation" where the learnings are based on life experience.
g) Plan field trips for enrichment.
h) Utilize multi-media to entertain and inform.
i) Include parents in the sharing sessions.
j) Include sessions on conflict resolution and management.

k) Develop decision making and problem solving skills.
l) Plan cooperatively developed projects.
m) Promote a business partnership among employers in the congregation.
n) Formulate a reading list, and help in research and speaking skills.
o) Develop a three tier program that begins 1) childhood (5-6th grade), 2) Tier 2, Childhood-Adolescent Passage (7-9th grade), 3) Tier 3, Adolescent-Young Adult Passage (10th- 12th grade).

H. Conclusion

The development of self and image among adolescents has led me to adopt the idea of "liberation partnerships" as a way of encouraging adolescent male maturation and mission. The partnership would work in two directions: It would allow adult men to begin the process of "generativity," sharing and passing their wisdom to the next generation; and second, the partnership would allow the adolescent a model and reference point from which conversation and evaluation could begin to take place.

Liberation partnership would allow both the adolescents and the adults to share their stories, pains, and fears. This liberation partnership in a Rite of Passage model has as its goal the integration and wholeness of the male adolescent's image. The partnership and the passage hopes to liberate both the adult and the adolescent to be free ***"for"*** each other without suspicion. I believe that this partnership is a step toward developing a healthy self.

This approach is an action approach. It is an alternative means for one adult and one adolescent to do something about adolescent development. This approach attempts to be layperson inclusive over against a professional staff of workers. It seeks to enlist many adults as partners who will stand in as models of responsibility for adolescent male growth.

The "mothers" of these adolescents helped to make the program work. Mothers were present and involved in the conversation and success of the program. I welcomed this participation because it brought a sensitivity, insight, and voice that is often not heard by adolescent males that is positive and encouraging.

A key to the success of this Rite of Passage is adult partners who are caring and willing to be vulnerable before adolescent males. The goal is exploration and reflection. I believe that this partnership can help adolescent males develop a "consciousness" of their being and personhood. I believe that it can be a step toward adolescents assuming their place and responsibility within the society. I also believe that this liberation educational model can serve as a tool to reshape the deformed image adolescents have assumed. It is hoped that pastors, parents, and church educators will work to develop a hermeneutic of interpretation to help adolescent males understand who they are in God and in the community of faith.

References & Annotated Bibliography

Barbour, C. Marie, Billman, Kathleen, DesJarlait, Peggy, and Doidge, Eleanor (1994). "Ministry on the Boundaries." In Susan Thistlethwaite and George Cairns (1994). Beyond Theological Tourism: Mentoring as a Grassroots Approach to Theological Education. Maryknoll, NY: Orbis Books.

Chapter 6 offers a method of praxis-based education that is transformative. The goal is to live in a mutual cooperation with people of other "social locations" with the goal of becoming partners with them through mutual engagements and boundary crossing experiences. The basic insights I gained from this study was the idea of partnership that is incarnational. The goal as it relates to adolescents is to "be with" them and to "listen to" them in ways that call for mutual respect.

Berkouwer, G.C. (1962). Man: The Image of God. Grand Rapids, MI: Wm.B. Eerdmans Publishing Company.

This volume looks at the Old and New Testament understandings of the concept of Image of God. It has useful references to the biblical understanding of the Christian being created in the image of Christ.

Bonhoeffer, Dietrich (1959). Creation and Fall: A Theological Interpretation of Genesis 1-3. New York, NY: The Macmillian Company.

Bonhoeffer offers a brief statement about the image of God being a creation in freedom. Humanity is the created representative of God on earth for others that is seen in relationship with others. The image of God is an "analogy of relationship" and dependence on the other, both God and man (See "Image of God on Earth," pp. 35-40).

Bromiley, Geoffrey (1985). Theological Dictionary of the New Testament. Grand Rapids, MI: Wm.B. Eerdmans Publishing Company.

This is a dictionary of Greek New Testament words. It is useful in understanding the background an origin of words in the biblical context and their historical and present usage.

Butler, Lee (1997). "Marked By Mercy." Sermon preached on Sunday, January 26, 1997 For Baptist Men's Day at the First Baptist Church, University Park, IL 60466.

This sermon challenged conspiracy and deficiency theories that have defined African American maleness. It called African American men to realize that they as all men are subject to sin, but are also subject to the mercy of God. The mercy God gives is a mercy of protection, a mercy of providence, and a mercy that allows us to build in desolate places. For a copy of this sermon, write the First Baptist Church, Audio Visual Ministry, 450 University Parkway, University Park, IL 60466 or call (708) 534-2242.

Cairns, George (1994). "The Theory and Practice of Transformative Education." In Susan Thistlethwaite and George Cairns (1994). Beyond Theological Tourism: Mentoring as a Grassroots Approach to Theological Education. Maryknoll, NY: Orbis Books.

Campbell, Joseph (1949). The Hero With a Thousand Faces. New York, NY: Princeton University Press.

This work is an extensive study of the development of the hero in mythic literature. The hero may be a lover, a warrior, a saint, or a tyrant. The book offers challenges that we must take if we are going transform and shape our time and culture for positive goods.

In chapter 5, Cairns offers a dialogical method as a way of establishing a ministry of mutuality between the socially privileged and the grass roots people of Uptown Chicago area. His method suggested to my project a way for adults to be immersed in grassroots involvements with adolescents who have often been marginalized.

Chestang, Leon W. (1992). *The Manhood Manual for African American Boys and Young Men.* Detroit, MI: Special Concepts, Inc.

This is a small volume that has as its purpose to reflect on needed areas of adolescent development as seen from one man's perspective. It challenges adults and parents to take greater responsibility in their children's development.

Cone, James (1991). *A Black Theology of Liberation*. Maryknoll, N.Y.: Orbis Books.

In chapter 5 "The Human Being in Black Theology," Cone examines historical and classical theories of the image of God and concludes that the image of God is the created freedom to not obey oppressive laws. It is the freedom to revolt against oppression. Thus, for Cone, black rebellion against oppression is a human act.

Cose, Ellis (1993). The Rage of the Privileged Class. New York, NY: Harper Collins Publishers, Inc.

This book is the chronicle of African American middle class persons who have realized that economic success in a dominant society does not equate to human success. It shares the testimonies and frustrations of the highly educated and wealthy stopped by a "glass ceiling." It shares the frustrations of those who are in major positions not being accepted as peers, but held in contempt and suspicion.

Davis, Harold (1995). Talks My Father Never Had With Me: Helping the Young Black Male Make it to Adulthood. Champaign, IL: KJAC Publishing.

Davis attempts to weave together scripture and common sense in a workbook style presentation to help parents, adult sponsors, and adolescent males examine areas that are not in school curriculum. It is designed as a life curriculum and that has as its focus a concern for the survival of African American adolescents. It is set up as digestible readings that call for contextual reflection by the reader.

Dean, Kenda C. (2004). Practicing Passion: Youth and the Quest for a Passionate Church. Grand Rapids, MI: Wm.B. Eerdmans Publishing Company.

This is an extraordinary book that examines the excitement and feelings of youth. It delves into the need of youth to be a part of a spiritual community that will challenge them to live beyond the ordinary and everyday experiences of their lives. Suggestions are offered on how churches can effectively include youth in the total work of the church.

Eybers, Howard (1991). Pastoral Care to Black South Africans. Atlanta, GA: Scholars Press.

This is an extraordinary study of South African male adolescent development from an Erikson theory base. Eybers examines the religious, social, and home context as the major problem of South African adolescent male non-maturation. He challenges parents and churches to develop a hermeneutic of interpretation for their sons to break them out of the generational cycle that has perpetuated their low esteem and loss of identity.

Freire, Paulo (1995). Pedagogy of the Oppressed. New York, NY: Continuum Publishing Company.

This is a book that offers methods whereby oppressed people can liberate themselves from oppressive conditions. It offers techniques whereby people can partner and mentor one another to think in transformative ways to establish liberation.

Fusco, Chris (2004). "1 in 4 boys in foster care get charged with crimes." Chicago Sun Times, 14 January 2004, 31.

This book is significant in that it offers a course of action to help the oppressed become the initiators of their own freedom. The idea of *partnership with the oppressed* is significant for this study as a method to facilitate adolescent male freedom, esteem and identity. It challenges others to join in the humanization of other people by being with them, helping them to dialogue, problem solve, and initiate actions for their own human recovery.

Gilligan, Carol (1993). In A Different Voice: Psychological Theory and Women's Development. Cambridge, MA: Harvard University Press.

This text examines the psychology of human development with an emphasis on relationships, and how women play a part in the man's life cycle and her own personal development in times of crisis and transition.

Gilmore, David G. (1990). Manhood in the Making: Cultural Concepts of Masculinity. New Haven, CT: Yale University Press.

This text examines world cultures who have identified aspects of what it means to be "an approved male in any society." The basic premise is that "men are made, not born." This fact is seen in the harsh and difficult initiatory rites adolescent males must go through in some societies to be labeled and accepted as a man. The book shares the good, the bad, and the ugly side of adolescent maturation processes around the world.

Goldingay, John. Models for Interpretation of Scripture. Grand Rapids, MI: Wm.B. Eerdmans Publishing Company, 1995.

This book is a book on methods in teaching, explaining, and telling the story of scripture. It is useful in giving the preacher of the gospel tools of communication to help young people grasp the meaning of the word of God as well as ways to apply it to their present context.

Great Transitions: Preparing Adolescents for a New Century (1995). New York, NY: Carnegie Corporation of New York.

This is an attempt of various educators to examine the difficulties adolescents and children are facing in society with the intent of developing proactive events to help parents, adults, and teachers encourage adolescents and children to succeed in the school and home context. The manual offers a variety of strategy whereby this process can take place.

Grossman, Kate (2004). "Schools pressured to dump bad students." Chicago Sun Times, 9 January 2004, 8.

The articles centers on principals in the Chicago Public Schools who have attempted to get rid of low scoring students to heighten their overall school's test scores to gain high rating.

Hale-Benson, Janice (1982). Black Children: Their Roots, Culture, and Learning Styles. Baltimore, MD: The John Hopkins University Press.

This book makes a study of African children's styles of learning that are associated with intense relational emphasis. She believes that African American children are taught to learn in the same style, and that schooling does not adhere to this method of relational learning. She challenges educators to be flexible in teaching Black children to meet their learning style thus teaching for success over against settling for their failure.

________. (1989). "Psychosocial Experiences." In Charles R. Foster and Grant S. Shockley eds.

(1989). Working with Black Youth. Nashville, TN: Abingdon Press.

In chapter 2 of this volume, Hale-Benson examines the psychological and sociological realities directly related to the educational system that results in "creating" disadvantaged children and youth who are black. She examines the inferior education that leads adolescents and children to fail, and thus she labels the society that perpetuates this injustice as a pariah institution. She further suggests ways adults and churches can combat the systemic structures that creates a "disadvantaged child."

Hardy, Edward (ed.) (1954). "Gregory of Nyssa: An Address on Religious Instruction." Christology of the Later Fathers. Philadelphia, PA: The Westminster Press.

This study attempts to gain a classical understanding of the concept of the image of God. Gregory of Nyssa purports that the image is one of created goodness. With that goodness is liberty and freedom to participate in what is good and to "resemble transcendent dignity." Gregory's concept of the image of God appears to be that of a representative image that humanity is created.

Hare, Nathan and Hare, Julia (1985). Bringing the Black Boy to Manhood: The Passage. San Francisco, CA: The Black Think Tank.

This small volume has been called the foundation for a rite of passage program for adolescent males. The authors examine the hostile social condition of adolescent males that have led them to destructive behaviors. They identify the absent father as a key to loss of identity among adolescent males and they offer a process whereby parents and other concerned adults can begin the recovery process through a rite of passage program.

Harris, James (1995). Preaching Liberation. Minneapolis, MN: Fortress Press.

In chapter 4 "Challenge and Conflict: Preaching and the Black Male," Harris examines the systemic problems that lead to male oppression and poor esteem. He states that the negative image of the black male historically has led to the destruction of the black family. He believes this destruction can be combated by preaching that enables black males to embrace an African worldview of unity, spirituality, and oneness. The conspiracy to do away with black men can be overcome by a message of encouragement and value of the black man to the community and the church.

Hill, Paul, Jr. (1992). Coming of Age: African American Male Rite of Passage. Chicago, IL: African American Images.

In this text, Hill explores the overwhelming facts of death in the African American male community that results from racism, homicide, suicide, drugs, and violence. His challenge is for black men to become pro-social and interactive with adolescent males through a rite of passage program that can maximize adolescent development in spite of the adverse and debilitating influences they face. Hill offers ten principles of African education (pp. 65-67) that can be used in the development of rite of passage program.

hooks, bell (1994). Teaching To Transgress: Education as the Practice of Freedom. New York, NY: Routledge.

bell hooks offers a pedagogy of liberation based on the work of Paulo Freire's theory of liberation as the process of reflection and action. She develops her own unique system of liberation through what she terms the "engaged voice." She challenges readers to not be passive but active in the engaging ideas of others. Her theory is significant in that it can be used as a model to encourage adolescents to be more vocal as it relates to their issues, insights, and understandings that are significant to them.

Hudnell, Rudolph (1996). "Marketing Scouting in the African American Community." Naperville, IL: Boy Scouts of America.

This is an article that points to the involvement of adult men in the development of adolescents through a scouting program that is Afrocentric in its orientation and presentation. The development of a Rite of Passage is suggested.

Killen, Patricia and DeBeer, John (1995). The Art of Theological Reflection. New York, NY: The Crossroad Publishing Co.

This text was helpful on helping to see the goal of a ministry project. The authors challenge the reader to use a method of correlation to reflect on five basic areas theology must consider in one's experience. Look at experience, its content and its meaning. Second, examine one's feelings from the experience and note answers, wisdom, and values that emerge; three, observe images and symbols that come to mind to help interpret the experience and the feelings; four, allow insight to come from the images leading to transformation; five, take action that is necessary for change.

Kunjufu, Jawanza (1984). Developing Positive Self-Images and Discipline in Black Children. Chicago, IL: African American Images.

Kunjufu examines the causes of low esteem centering on mis-education in six areas: home and parents, the peer group, television and media, the school, the church, and the socio-economic influences. He suggests a more relational model of interaction with children to help build esteem and identity in them over against a linear model that sees them as objects to be acted upon. He offers suggestions to parents and teachers on how motivation can be done to change children's self-attitude and performance.

________ (1985). Countering the Conspiracy to Destroy Black Boys. Chicago, IL: African American Images.

The conspiracy theory is based on institutional racism and white supremacy within educational systems. He asks, "How can children who come to the class with innocence, trust, and an enthusiasm to learn, and please, lose that excitement?" Kunjufu notes that the educative environment changes from "a socially interactive style to a competitive, individualistic, and minimally socially interactive style of learning." The lack of continuity in teaching, poor teaching styles, teachers that don't care, and a lack of male teachers and presence, and the media contribute to the drop out and push out rate of black boys. This begins for Kunjufu in the fourth grade. He offers a rite of passage program as a way to educate African American males for liberation and the maximizing of human potential.

________ (1986). Countering the Conspiracy to Destroy Black Boys Vol. 2. Chicago, IL: African American Images.

In this volume, Kunjufu offers strategies parents can use to develop responsibility in boys. He describes a need for the adult males presence to educate boys on sexual responsibility. He examines the dialectical relationship of male students to female teachers and how to help boys succeed instead of fail in school through what he terms "a relevant curriculum." Finally, Kunjufu offers a Rite of Passage program as essential in brings boys to manhood.

________ (1986). Motivating and Preparing Black Youth for Success. Chicago, IL: African American Images.

In this text, Kunjufu examines the relationship between economics and racism. He states that self-esteem and determination has been tied to the economy where many blacks are locked out. To achieve success, one must change one's system of values (see pp. 23-24). Kunjufu states that adolescent success is determined by them understanding racism, by them knowing who they are, by discipline, time management, vision, patience, giving them options and alternatives, work and career development.

________ (1988). To Be Popular or Smart: The Black Peer Group. Chicago, IL: African American Images.

This text challenges its readers to be free of the historical social bondage of inferiority. The call is to redefine blackness from a "pro African" frame of mind (pre-encounter, encounter, immersion, internalization, commitment). This model should transcend a victim-loser analysis. Teachers and parents should move from strictly a "grade concern" to "goal and value" concern to motivate children and adolescents. He offers suggestions how the community can demonstrate an atmosphere of learning that motivates success in children and adolescents.

________ (1989). Critical Issues in Educating African American Youth. Chicago, IL: African American Images.

Kunjufu explores areas he sees as the contributing factors in school failure or success: teacher expectation, tracking, parental involvement, student self-esteem, curriculum, learning styles, test bias, and peer pressure. In his chapter on "Black Boys" (pp. 53-61), there are suggestions on how to develop adult male and adolescent male relationships along with a Rite of Passage program to bring adolescents to adulthood.

________ (1990). Countering the Conspiracy to Destroy Black Boys Vol. III. Chicago, IL: African American Images.

In this volume, Kunjufu attempts to examine African American males by age. In his groupings, he seeks to show the basic needs at each level and the corrections that are necessary for growth and development. In chapter 2 (pp. 27-43), he describes the loss of interaction and parental involvement, no concern for learning styles, peer pressure, and low teacher expectations. One remedy offered to male school failure is the "Black male classroom" (see pp. 37-38). Chapter 3 is on "Adolescents." To help adolescents, Kunjufu suggests that this age group (13-18) be challenged in problem solving and critical thinking with a curriculum that is more multicultural and Afrocentric. He states that the teacher relationship should be more *coach* over against *instructor*.

Mandela, Nelson (1994). Long Walk To Freedom. New York, NY: Little, Brown, and Company.

This is the autobiography of Nelson Mandela. The significance of this work is Mandela's recalling of his initiation into manhood through his tribe's rite of passage. The story of his rite of passage experience is told in chapter 4 pages 22-27. Mandela says, "Now I was a man, and I would never again…drink milk from a cow's udder. I was already in mourning for my own youth. Looking back, I know that I was not a man that day and would not truly become one for many years (p. 27).

Mitchell, Henry and Thomas, Emil (1994). Preaching for Black Self-Esteem. Nashville, TN: Abingdon Press.

This volume shares the systemic destructive racial history behind low esteem and shame within the African American context as it regards physical features and mental intelligence. It suggests ways the African American preacher can contribute to esteem building through preaching. This method suggests using an Afrocentric hermeneutic that interprets the scripture through one's experience of struggle, the hope of liberation, and the vision of the kingdom of equality and justice.

Mitchell, Mary (2005). "Black Murder Stat Doubtful, but Cause for Alarm Anyway." Chicago Sun Times, 25 August 2005, 10.

Moore, Robert and Gillette Douglas (1990). King, Warrior, Magician, Lover: Rediscovering the Archetypes of the Mature Masculine. New York, NY: Harper Collins Publishers.

Moore and Gillette examine issues facing adolescent maturation into adult responsibility. They offer significant reasons for the development of ritual and rite of passage programs for adolescent development and growth. For persons working with youth, their chapter on "From Boy Psychology to Man Psychology" is worthy of examination in the light of present male difficulties today.

________ (1992). The Warrior Within: Accessing the Knight in the Male Psyche. New York, NY: William Morrow and Company, Inc.

This text attempts to understand the element in the male psyche that works toward the protection of the community. This text is useful in understanding male aggression and how it can be used for world building purposes.

_________ (1993). The Magician Within: Accessing the Shaman in the Male Psyche. New York, NY: William Morrow and Company, Inc.

This text examines the psyche of the thinker energy within us. The magician is not a trickster, but a person who uses his/her mind and thinking process to initiate people into responsible adulthood. This aspect of the psyche is the mentor who helps us navigate through the crazy times, the crisis times, and the trauma times of our lives to build a life giving and a life sustaining world.

Parham, Thomas (1993). Psychological Storms: The African American Struggle for Identity. Chicago, IL: African American Images.

This reading examines a theory for African Americans to be de-culturized and revitalized from anti-Black feelings to self-pride and pro-Blackness (pp. 37-43). He also charts value systems between Whites and Blacks and asks readers to identify areas of conflict where anxiety and fear often arise in their identity.

Pearson, Carol (1989). The Hero Within: Six Archetypes We Live By. New York, NY: Harper Collins Publishers.

This work is a study of the archetypal structures of the mind that make us the persons that we are becoming. The key concept of the text is how to become a hero in each phase of our life journey. The key idea is that a hero is a person who takes responsibility for his/her self and for others with the aim of transformation and revival.

Rampersad, Arnold (1994). "Afterward." In Richard Wright (1994). <u>Rite of Passage</u>. New York, NY: Harper Trophy.

This novella, as it is categorized, is a telling story by Richard Wright of a young man who becomes a gang member and a gang leader. It shares the psychology of the gang, its loyalties, and family orientations. It points to one black child's transition into manhood.

Roeper, Richard (2005). "Too Many Rappers Dying for a Shot at Fame." <u>Chicago Sun Times</u>, 30 August 2005, 11.

In this article Roeper points to the high price some young men have paid trying to immolate the thug life to make it big as rap stars. The thug life has led many of them to an early grave.

Seymour, Jack, and Miller, Donald et al (1982). Contemporary Approaches to Christian Education. Nashville, TN: Abingdon Press.

This text offers approaches to teach young people how to develop and grow their faith in Jesus Christ. Those who work with young people will gain fresh insights as to procedures and processes that can be used to develop the next generation in the faith.

Smith, Efrem (2004). Raising Up Young Heroes: Developing A Revolutionary Youth Ministry. Downers Grove, IL: InterVarsity Press.

This text offers biblical and practical methods of moving a youth group to a revolutionary group that seeks to establish love, justice, and grace in the context where youth find themselves. This book utilizes a holistic approach verses a program approach in developing youth to be champions for Christ in their social context.

Tillich, Paul (1967). Systematic Theology Vol. 1: Three Volumes in One. Chicago, IL: The University of Chicago Press.

Tillich is important because of his method of correlation (see Vol. 1 pp. 59ff, Vol. 2 pp. 59ff). This method is useful in that it helps answer the question of how adults and adolescents can work together to create in each a "new being" (see Vol. 2 pp. 118ff). Tillich is valuable in his idea of the image of God. Humanity seeks self-actualization and being. Self-actualization is applicable to the African American struggle for liberation and actualization of being in a social structure that fights against it (see Vol. 1 pp. 258ff).

Thomas, Laurence M. (1993). Vessels of Evil: American Slavery and the Holocaust. Philadelphia, PA: Temple University Press.

Thomas gives the social history of victimization of African Americans during slavery that resulted in problems of sexism, moral devaluation, cooperative subordination, and internalized norms of the oppressors experienced today. As a result of the brutality, there is alienation of historical-cultural traditions and the loss of self-identity. He points out that this victimization has led to psychological developments of self-hatred which is related to the urban violence today (see chapter 6 "American Slavery and the Holocaust" and chapter 7 "Murderous Extermination and Natal Alienation").

Turner, Victor (1995). The Ritual Process. Hawthorne, NY: Aldine De Gruyter.

The benefit of this book is Turner's discussion of the Rite of Passage as a "liminal" and in-between experience for the initiant. Turner offered me a basic understanding of oppression as it relates to adolescent males. The process of detachment, separation, and loss, which is a process he describes as a phase into a rite of passage, is in fact, an experience of African American males when they reach adolescence. The culture and society initiates them into a "nobody state." Turner is useful in his examination of the stages of most cultures process of a rite being "separation, the liminal period, and the reincorporation (See pp. 94-96).

Waters, Kenneth L. (1993). "Made in God's Image." Afrocentric Sermons. Valley Forge, PA: Judson Press.

In his sermon, Waters poses the argument that our relationship and responsibility to one another is based on our human reality of sociality. God is a social being and we are created in that same image. This image of social relationships challenges us to relate meaningfully to one another, helping one another achieve full potential and being.

West, Cornel (1994). Races Matters. New York, NY: Vintage Books.

This text offers a historical and contemporary examination of the systemic structural constraints that led to the oppression of African Americans. West identifies what he terms the "nihilistic threat." This "threat" is the result of systemic victimization and has led to depression, worthlessness, despair. His solution to the "threat" is the 1) use of "moral reasoning" that denounces victimization of all people, 2) a "prophetic moral assessment" that points to dignity and critiques the "powers that be" and puts forward a vision of fundamental social change, 3) a coalition that struggles against racism, 4) and a black cultural democracy that liberates all people.

Whitehead, James and Whitehead, Evelyn (1995). Method in Ministry. Kansas City, MO: Sheed & Ward.

This text offers foundations for theological reflection. The authors suggest a method of correlation that asks questions of reflection from one's context of ministry (pastoral, jail ministry, etc.). It asks how one's experiences relate to the context and what answers can that context offer? The next step is to repeat the process asking how one's tradition/scriptures can bring significant reflection on the context. The next correlation and conversation is with the culture/social sciences; it asks how various disciplines affect one's ministry initiatives? From these stages assertions are ascertained and a response must be made as to insights and actions that will be taken into account.

Wright, Richard (1994). Rite of Passage. New York, NY: Harper Trophy.

This novella is the story of foster boys who are left behind by the foster care system. They leave their childhood behind and take to the streets in gang activity for survival. This is a story that examines the condition of black males and their search for a place in the family and society.

Wright, Roosevelt (1994). Where are the Black Men? Monroe, LA: Free Press Publishers.

This volume is concerned with the disappearance of the African American adult male in the religious and civic context. The challenge is for adult males to become models in crisis, relationships, and faith for adolescents to follow. To recover men, Wright offers suggestions that the church, civil organizations, and home can do to challenge men to greater responsibility with adolescent males. One model that is advocated is the scouting model where men and boys can join together in planned activities for growth and development.

Yust, Karen (2004). Real Kids, Real Faith: Practices for Nurturing Children's Spiritual Lives. San Francisco, CA: Jossey-Bass.

Yust offers teachers of children and youth key ideas that help shape faith. Her basic premise has to do with nurturing and developing the faith that children already have by being a part of the community of faith. Faith grows and develops among the people of faith. She encourages the importance of children and youth going to church to learn through observation what it means to be a person of faith who is faithful.

Appendix A

INTRODUCTION: WHAT IS A RITE OF PASSAGE?

WELCOME TO THE FIRST BAPTIST CHURCH RITE OF PASSAGE PROGRAM. WHEREVER CIVILIZED CULTURES HAVE LIVED, THERE HAVE EXISTED RITES AND RITUALS TO COMMEMORATE THE PASSAGE OF ADOLESCENTS INTO ADULTHOOD.

A RITE OF PASSAGE PROGRAM IS A WAY FOR AN ADOLESCENT TO GAIN SELF IDENTITY. IT IS A WAY TO KNOW WHEN AND WHERE A TRANSITION INTO ADULT AND SOCIAL RESPONSIBILITY HAS TAKEN PLACE. THE RITUALS WILL ATTEMPT TO GIVE THE ADOLESCENT A SPECIAL QUALITY, PURPOSE, FUNCTION, AND CONNECTEDNESS TO GOD.

THE BENEFITS:

IT IS HOPED THAT EACH ADOLESCENT WILL GAIN A POSITIVE SENSE OF SELF AS EXPERIENCED IN A FELLOWSHIP OF CHRISTIAN MEN AND THE STUDY OF THE BIBLE.

EXPECTED OUTCOMES:

1. TO COMPLETE THE PROGRAM
2. TO NOT BE INFLUENCED IN GANGS OR CRIMINAL ACTIVITY
3. TO GAIN A HIGHER SCHOLASTIC COMPETENCE AT SCHOOL
4. TO DEMONSTRATE LEADERSHIP AT HOME, SCHOOL, CHURCH, AND COMMUNITY.
5. TO GAIN A VOCATIONAL AND EDUCATIONAL VISION.

GETTING STARTED

REQUIREMENTS FOR THE PROGRAM

1. EACH ADOLESCENT IS ASKED TO PARTICIPATE IN THE CHURCH'S ***SATURDAY OR SUNDAY BIBLE STUDY*** TO GAIN THE BIBLICAL BASE NEEDED FOR GOD'S VISION & PURPOSE.

2. EACH ADOLESCENT IS ASKED TO PARTICIPATE IN THE ***FIRST BAPTIST YOUTH ACTIVITIES.***

3. SIGN THE ***PARENT & STUDENT AGREEMENT*** TO PARTICIPATE.

4. PARENTS & INITIANT IS TO HAVE A 15 MINUTE INTERVIEW WITH THE PASTOR

(WHAT ARE YOUR PERCEPTIONS OF YOUR SON ABILITIES AND YOUR EXPECTATION FOR HIM).

5. ***MAIL A PREPARED LETTER*** (SIGNED BY THE PASTOR & ADOLESCENT) ***TO YOUR SCHOOL PRINCIPAL*** NOTIFYING HIM OR HER OF YOUR PARTICIPATION IN THIS RITE OF PASSAGE PROGRAM.

6. GET A LETTER OF RECOMMENDATION FROM ***YOUR SCHOOL DEAN***.

7. GET A LETTER OF RECOMMENDATION FROM ***A DEACON/ELDER*** OF THE CHURCH.

Appendix B

Student Evaluations of the Program

1. What were the most important learning's in the program for you?

Robert: "The most important learning I gained was how to see the world differently. At first, I didn't care what was happening in the world. I was only looking out for my family and me, but now I know what happens in the world affects me. As a result, I will take charge of my actions and affect the actions around me."

Rickey: "The African American poetry was significant to me."

Greg: "I learned about responsibility and seeing and understanding the views of others."

2. Complete the following statement: "I am…"

Greg: "I am intelligent, successful, a leader, not a follower of anyone except God."

Rickey: "I am a very special person. God has something planned for me in the future. God wants me to be a leader."

Robert: "I am a Black African American youth. I am loving, caring, and understanding. I show leadership in activities both in the community and church. I am a person who will try to make a difference in his home, school, and even the world. I love to see positive Black males who are making a difference. I look up to those leaders and try to follow in their footsteps. As I grow and become a man, I will try my best to be a role model to upcoming youth."

3. Tell how this program can be improved.

Greg: "More involvement, more activities, make the boys more visible."

Rickey: "Get the men of the church to go out and reach other young boys on the streets to be drawn to Christ."

Robert: "Instead of meeting once a week, meet twice a week. Plan more activities."

Appendix C

Parent Evaluation of the Program

1. In what way has the program been helpful to your son?

Mariah: "He is aware of others feelings, less argumentative. He is beginning to wash and iron his own clothes and cook."

Janette: "My son is becoming somewhat more responsible in the chores he does. He has become more strong about who he is in Christ."

Michael: The program was helpful because it forced us to have discussion we probably would not have. It helped us both develop a better understanding of each other.

2. What changes have you seen in your son since he has been in the program?

Mariah: "He is more responsible, more mature, less selfish, and is more concerned about others. He is controlling his tongue better."

Janette: "He is talking about goals and sharing what he has received from the program."

Michael: "He is beginning to mature more."

3. In what way was your involvement with him during the process helpful?

Mariah: "I began encouraging him more. As a result of the program, I began giving him more responsibility."

Janette: "During the program, I let him know that through Christ all things are possible. I told him to keep what he has learned through the program near his heart and learn from it."

Michael: I like having to go somewhere with him on a regular basis. Discussions in the car became very powerful and it forced quiet time together."

Appendix D

Council of Elders Evaluation of the Program

1. **How was the program helpful to our adolescent boys?**

- It focused on the necessity and value of spiritual growth and development, responsibility, and leadership.
- The program showed the young men a man's perspective on a variety of issues. The program helped the boys to know some of what men feel and believe.
- The program provided a spiritual framework for adolescent boys. The adult mentoring was an excellent idea because of the male role model which is so badly needed in our society, especially with African American adolescents.
- This program communicated to the boys our pastor's and church's concern that they become "men of God." It also helped them to see that they are a priority at least to some of the men.

2. **What should the outcome of a program like this produce in boys?**

- Leadership skills
- Spiritual connectedness

- Decision making/problem solving skills
- Strong sons of self-worth
- It should produce a young man with insight regarding a variety of issues. It should also give these young men some history which helps to produce a better understanding on a lot of different subjects.
- This program should produce an awareness of each individual's need to develop a positive self image. It should also create an awareness of who they are. By utilizing the adult mentors, these young adolescents can identify with some of the conflicts that we encountered as we were growing up, thus creating an understanding that problems can be solved and conflicts can be resolved.
- This program should become a staple experience in three tiers which seeks to inculcate character, knowledge content, and skills which will enable our boys to excel regardless of the challenges they will face: 1. Tier 1—childhood, 2. Tier 2—childhood - adolescent passage, 3. Tier 3—Adolescent - Young Adult Passage aimed at maturing into manhood.

3. What aspects should be added to make it relevant and meaningful to the boys?

- Cooperative projects (2-3 boys working together). Focus on specific aspects of the program where each young man is assigned a role or assumes a role for him to carry out as his contribution to the whole.

- Develop more hands on projects to the program. They should have projects that they are to complete as groups under direct adult supervision.
- I think it is important for adolescents to understand conflict resolution. We must begin to instill in our young adolescents the need to set goals and also start to put material things in the right perspective.
- Lesson planning should aim at making theoretical information practical.
- Homework assignments should be a project oriented life application.
- All homework should be done as a group project.
- More field trips should be planned to accent the cultural/historical dimensions.

4. List ways to improve the program.

- Develop a business partnership.
- Develop and implement a recruitment program.
- Develop feedback mechanisms for the young men who have participated in the program.
- Add more hands on projects that require both individual and group effort. Both sets of projects should be adult non-supervised and supervised.
- The young men should read a book a month and report on it.
- The program was too concentrated and intense. Extend the program over a longer period of time with fewer meetings to one a month. This would allow us to evaluate whether the training is being effective.

- Team the boys up to go on the job with the men earlier in the program and have them report on their experience to the group.
- Insist that parents also become a part of this program. They may be limited in the amount of time they can devote, however if they can attend only one session, it will be helpful. A particular topic might be: "Accepting Parental Responsibility In Today's Society."
- Instill in our youngsters the need to become educated; know your history. They need to understand that Africans had a history before slavery. Somehow we need to get through to them that our history is not from "Slavery to Ghetto."
- Repackage information utilizing multi-media avenues of presentation to their visual perception and their maturational processes.

Appendix E

The Rite of Passage Graduation Ceremony Sunday, June 16, 1996 11:00 a.m.

Hymn "Rise Up O Men O God"

Rise up, O men of God!/ Have done with lesser things;/Give heart and mind and soul and strength/ To serve the King of Kings.

Rise up, O men of God! The church for you doth wait,/ Her strength unequal to her task;/ Rise up and make her great!

Responsive Reading

Leader: I pray for them, I am not praying for the world, but for those you have given me, for they are yours. And glory has come to me through them.

People: Hold Father, protect them by the power of your name…so that they may be one.

All: My prayer is not that you take them out of the world, but that you protect them from the evil one (Jn. 17:9-11).

Occasion Bro. Michael Spight

Genesis 1:26 says, “Let us make man in our image and likeness.” God calls the church to make boys and girls into men and women. Our church has developed a Rite of Passage Program to encourage adolescent boys to gain self-identity as to what it means to be a man created in the image of Christ.

This rite of passage is a mark where an adolescent male can have a way of transitioning into young adulthood and the social responsibilities that comes with it. The goal of this church based program is to give adolescent boys a sense of sacredness of self, purpose, responsibility, and adult commitment as social beings.

The expected outcome of this program is to encourage adolescent boys to stay out of gangs and to stay in school and the church. It expects the boys to gain higher academic competence to meet the challenges of a technological world. It expects the boys to exhibit leadership at home, school, church, and in the community. It expects the boys to be respectful toward self, others, parents, and God. It expects the boys to gain a vocational vision for the future for which they are called now to prepare.

The Presentation of the Candidates Pastor R. Jackson

All Council of Elders and Men Who Worked With These Boys,
Come Forward And Stand Behind Them.

Randy Bell	Chris Evans	Greg Hill	Malcom Williams
Rickey Hawkins	Van K. Johnson	Kortez McTeer	Ricky Purifoy
William Reed	Robert Slaughter		

The Prayer of Dedication Rev. Stanley Williams

The Stole Presentation The Council of Elders

The Pin Presentation The Parents

The Sermon ***Dr. Kenneth Smith***
President, Chicago Theological Seminary

Invitation to Discipleship Benediction

Appendix F

From Darkness to Light: Who Am I?

The movement from childhood to adulthood is a period of confusion, or "darkness" as the young person searches for the light of who they are as persons. To begin the move to the light, the following surveys have been established to help the mentor and the young person begin dialoging on the nature of the young person's identity. Take the following pages and use them as teaching tools to address the need and the search for answer of the question – "Who am I?" (***All of the responses to the surveys are "yes." Discuss with the survey participants why they chose different answers).***

Who is a Hero?

Check the box that gives your understanding of a hero. Discuss Bible stories that point to the ideas listed below.

1. **A Hero is life-giving and gives healing power (Read Mark 9:14-29).**
   Yes ☐ No ☐ Uncertain ☐

2. **A Hero is one who has been tested and passed the test.**
   Yes ☐ No ☐ Uncertain ☐

3. **A Hero is one who "faces and kills the dragon-terrors," the "tyrant-monsters."**
   Yes ☐ No ☐ Uncertain ☐

4. **The hero is one who submits to a difficult task for others.**
   Yes ☐ No ☐ Uncertain ☐

5. **The hero is limited but battles past limitations to inspire others.**
   Yes ☐ No ☐ Uncertain ☐

6. **The hero goes into the world to transform it, renew it, and makes it a holy place.**
   Yes ☐ No ☐ Uncertain ☐

7. A Hero is not a super star athlete or a pop star with money and a big name.

Yes ☐ No ☐ Uncertain ☐

8. A Hero is a father, an uncle, a grandfather, a man who does not abandon or run out on his family.

Yes ☐ No ☐ Uncertain ☐

9. A hero is a man who will love, sacrifice, and gives what he has to better his family.

Yes ☐ No ☐ Uncertain ☐

10. A hero is a life-giver who offers himself sacrificially to build a better world for those who come after him.

Yes ☐ No ☐ Uncertain ☐

11. A Hero is one who brings light, understanding, and enlightenment to the mind and soul.

Yes ☐ No ☐ Uncertain

12. A Hero is one who will not turn back regardless of the difficulty of the task.

Yes ☐ No ☐ Uncertain ☐

13. The hero overcomes his self-interests to revitalize the world.

Yes ☐ No ☐ Uncertain ☐

Who are My Biblical & Social Heroes?

Write at least two persons that are your Bible Heroes and tell what makes them a hero.

1. My biblical hero.

This person is my Bible hero because

2. My first Social hero. ______________________________

This person is my social hero because.

My Self-Identity: Socially

Check the box that best describes what it means to be a self (person).
Discuss each of the following. Share Bible stories that may relate to each experience.

1. I am defined by my ability, skill, or talent.
   Yes ☐ **No** ☐ **Uncertain** ☐

2. I feel good about myself because I have it all together.
   Yes ☐ **No** ☐ **Uncertain** ☐

3. My appearance and good looks defines who I am to others.
   Yes ☐ **No** ☐ **Uncertain** ☐

4. My status, accomplishments, and recognition of others make me somebody.
   Yes ☐ **No** ☐ **Uncertain** ☐

5. The admiration of others, gives me a sense of self worth.
   Yes ☐ **No** ☐ **Uncertain** ☐

6. My social status verifies that I am somebody.
   Yes ☐ **No** ☐ **Uncertain** ☐

7. When I am criticized, feel guilty, or fearful, I feel like I am worthless.
Yes ▢ **No** ▢ **Uncertain** ▢

8. Climbing the ladder of success will lead me to happiness.
Yes ▢ **No** ▢ **Uncertain** ▢

9. My happiness is equal to my good looks and what I have in the bank.
Yes ▢ **No** ▢ **Uncertain** ▢

10. I see myself as a failure.
Yes ▢ **No** ▢ **Uncertain** ▢

11. Nobody really likes me.
Yes ▢ **No** ▢ **Uncertain** ▢

12. I have a lot of guilt and shame in my life.
Yes ▢ **No** ▢ **Uncertain** ▢

My Self-Identity: Biblically

Check the box that best describes what it means to be a self (person).
Discuss each of the following. Share Bible stories that may relate to each experience.

1. I have had a life changing experience in Jesus.
   Yes ☐ **No** ☐ **Uncertain**

2. I am a forgiven person.
   Yes ☐ **No** ☐ **Uncertain**

3. Who I am is not predicated on what I have or don't have. **Yes** ☐ **No** ☐ **Uncertain**

4. My identity is found in the work of God's kingdom.
   Yes ☐ **No** ☐ **Uncertain**

5. I am significant with a divine purpose.
   Yes ☐ **No** ☐ **Uncertain**

6. I belong to God. **Yes** ☐ **No** ☐ **Uncertain**

7. I am the salt of the earth (Mt. 5:13).
   Yes ☐ **No** ☐ **Uncertain**

8. I am the light of the world (Mt. 5:14).
   Yes ☐ **No** ☐ **Uncertain**

9. I am a child of God (Jn 1:12).
Yes ▢ **No** ▢ **Uncertain**

10. I am Christ's friend (Jn 15:15).
Yes ▢ **No** ▢ **Uncertain**

11. I am appointed to bear Christ's fruit (Jn 15:16).
Yes ▢ **No** ▢ **Uncertain**

12. I am God's slave (Rom. 6:22).
Yes ▢ **No** ▢ **Uncertain**

13. I am a joint heir with Christ (Rom. 8:17).
Yes ▢ **No** ▢ **Uncertain**

14. I am God's temple (1 Cor. 3:16).
Yes ▢ **No** ▢ **Uncertain**

15. I am a minister of reconciliation (2 Cor. 5:18, 19).
Yes ▢ **No** ▢ **Uncertain**

16. I am a saint (Eph. 1:1). **Yes** ▢ **No** ▢ **Uncertain**

17. I am God's handiwork (Eph. 2:10).
Yes ▢ **No** ▢ **Uncertain**

18. I am chosen of God and dearly loved (Col. 3:12).
Yes ▢ **No** ▢ **Uncertain**

19. I am a son of light not darkness (1 Thess. 5:5).
Yes ▢ **No** ▢ **Uncertain**

20. I am a member of a royal priesthood (1 Pet. 2:9, 10). **Yes** ▢ **No** ▢ **Uncertain**

21. I am an enemy of the devil (1 Pet. 5:8).
    Yes ▢ **No** ▢ **Uncertain**

22. I am what I am by the grace of God (1 Cor. 15:10).
    Yes ▢ **No** ▢ **Uncertain**

My Self-Identity: Theologically

Check the box that best describes what it means to be a self (person).
Discuss each of the following. Share Bible stories that may relate to each experience.

1. I am a *dynamic* and expanding person. Who I am today will change and be different tomorrow.
   Yes ☐ **No** ☐ **Uncertain**

2. I am multi-dimensional person. I am constantly changing and moving towards growth.
   Yes ☐ **No** ☐ **Uncertain**

3. I am *self-aware*. I am shaped by others, but I am more than what I presently seem to be.
   Yes ☐ **No** ☐ **Uncertain**

4. I am *multidimensional.* Psalm 139:14-16 point to us being "wonderfully made."
   Yes ☐ **No** ☐ **Uncertain**

5. I understand that I am a "definite center."
   Yes ☐ **No** ☐ **Uncertain**

6. As a *personal self*, I am my own starting point.
   Yes ☐ **No** ☐ **Uncertain**

7. I am a person who can *fall apart*. As a participant with others, I can lose my identity tying to be like others. **Yes ▢ No ▢ Uncertain**

8. I am *impressed* by others. I receive overpowering impressions from others that impact me and impress me. **Yes ▢ No ▢ Uncertain**

9. I am a *responsible moral person* who has the power to participate in a community of others bringing healing and hope. **Yes ▢ No ▢ Uncertain**

10. I am a person who experiences self-sacrifice, the "give and take" of life. **Yes ▢ No ▢ Uncertain**

11. I am a *dynamic creative* person who moves beyond my limits. **Yes ▢ No ▢ Uncertain**

12. I am a person who has the power *determine and shape my destination.* **Yes ▢ No ▢ Uncertain**

13. I am *"other-determined."* The person that I am and will become depends on the actions of other persons who relate to me directly or indirectly.
Yes ▢ No ▢ Uncertain